Survey Design and Analysis using TURBOSTATS

CW00693941

For my family, both in England and in Mexico

Survey Design and Analysis using TURBOSTATS

Mike Hart

Department of Public Policy and Managerial Studies
De Montfort University
Leicester
UK

CHAPMAN & HALL
University and Professional Division
London · Glasgow · New York · Tokyo · Melbourne · Madras

Published by Chapman & Hall, 2–6 Boundary Row, London SE1 8HN

Chapman & Hall, 2–6 Boundary Row, London SE1 8HN, UK

Blackie Academic & Professional, Wester Cleddens Road, Bishopbriggs, Glasgow G64 2NZ, UK

Chapman & Hall Inc., 29 West 35th Street, New York NY10001, USA

Chapman & Hall Japan, Thomson Publishing Japan, Hirakawacho Nemoto Building, 6F, 1-7-11 Hirakawa-cho, Chiyoda-ku, Tokyo 102, Japan

Chapman & Hall Australia, Thomas Nelson Australia, 102 Dodds Street, South Melbourne, Victoria 3205, Australia

Chapman & Hall India, R. Seshadri, 32 Second Main Road, CIT East, Madras 600 035, India

First edition 1993

© 1993 Mike Hart

Typeset in 10/12 pt Palatino by Falcon Graphic Art, Wallington, Surrey
Printed in Great Britain by St Edmundsbury Press, Bury St Edmunds, Suffolk

ISBN 0 412 54830 5

A catalogue record for this book is available from the British Library

Library of Congress Cataloging-in-Publication data

Hart, Mike.
  Survey design and analysis using TURBOSTATS / Mike Hart. – 1st ed.
      p.   cm.
  Includes bibliographical references and index.
  ISBN 0–412–54830–5
  1. TURBOSTATS.   2. Surveys – Methodology – Computer programs.
3. Social sciences – Statistical methods – Computer programs.
I. Title.
HA31.2.H36   1993
001.4'33—dc20

∞ Printed on permanent acid-free text paper, manufactured in accordance
  with the proposed ANSI/NISO Z 39.48-199X and ANSI Z 39.48-1984

Contents

Preface

This book is intended as a very practical guide to the process of conducting a social survey. It contains a statistical suite of programs, TURBOSTATS, specifically designed for survey analysis. Many modern books on survey design refer readers to the computer packages they might use for their analysis but this book is probably unique in that it supplies a fully functional statistical system which can be used with any version of the MS-DOS operating system for the IBM PC (or PC-compatible) range of personal computers.

The text is written for the use of all those practitioners in a variety of functions in both the private and the public sectors who need to conduct a survey by questionnaire. It should prove particularly useful for the busy personnel who have only the occasional, but none the less, urgent need to obtain and process survey results rapidly. By using the software provided, it is possible to get professional results in a reasonably short space of time and without the long 'learning curve' that would otherwise be required. Experienced researchers probably have superior tools at their disposal already but they, too, should find the book of interest. Students on a range of higher education courses are often encouraged to undertake survey work as part of their project work or undergraduate dissertation. I hope that this book will be particularly useful for them, not only in their academic work but also when they enter employment, either as part of a sandwich degree or upon graduation.

The output of the TURBOSTATS system follows quite closely that given by the most widely used survey analysis package, SPSS (Statistical Package for the Social Sciences). In particular, the output of the frequencies and cross-tabulation programs are almost identical. The TURBOSTATS programs are not the same size or as complex as SPSS but they will perform the types of analyses that are most often needed in questionnaire and survey analysis more than adequately.

An assumption throughout this book is that readers need to undertake some survey research but time and resources are limited. As questionnaires are the most widely used method for the collection of data, this book confines its attention to the analysis of data collected by this method. Very often, results are needed 'yesterday' but a rushed job runs the risk of containing fundamental flaws which can undermine its validity and credibility. By following the advice contained in these pages, the user should be able to avoid elementary errors and be able to produce a workmanlike survey that stands up to critical examination.

This book is intended as a short, practical guide and I would suggest that readers attempt to read the first three chapters fairly quickly at one sitting to get an overview of the whole before starting to study the individual techniques required in more detail. It is probable, however, that readers may like to refer to other sources to deepen their knowledge. An annotated bibliography of a few useful books on social survey analysis and statistics is given in Appendix C.

It is customary to extend thanks to the various individuals who have helped a project to fruition. I would like therefore to thank the several generations of students who for several years now have used the TURBOSTATS package in their project work at De Montfort University, Leicester (formerly Leicester Polytechnic). When they encountered the occasional difficulty, it was sometimes possible to refine the programming of the package or to frame advice on how to avoid similar difficulties in the future. Particular thanks are due to Leticia Gaeta Gonzalez and the *Leicester Environment City* campaign team for permission to reproduce the sample questionnaire in Appendix G. Two of my colleagues at De Montfort University, Pete Lowe and Simon Dyson, have made valuable comments upon the first draft of the text. Thanks are also due to my son, Martin, for some valuable suggestions from the perspective of the research practitioner. A final and special word of thanks must go to my wife, Meg, who was deprived of so much of my time and company whilst the text and programs were in the course of preparation and refinement. Whatever faults remain are, of course, my own.

'Let's do a survey!'   1

INTRODUCTION

The social survey is now a part of our everyday life. Whether we are stopped in the street by an interviewer, complete with clipboard, or we read the latest opinion poll in our newspapers, then we know that some organization or other is 'doing a survey'. The survey method is increasingly being used in both schools and colleges in project work as a way of introducing students to the practicalities of social research. In Britain at the moment, there are increasing examples of 'consumer satisfaction surveys' in which the views of the public are actively sought in order to deliver quality in the provision of goods and services.

Some would argue that using surveys frequently and, perhaps, indiscriminately is bringing the whole of the survey method into disrepute. Indeed, the very fact that surveys are so commonplace may well give rise to a certain cynicism when the results of a survey are announced. When the results are in accordance with public expectations, voices will be heard to make the remark that 'they didn't need a survey to tell them that', whilst if the results seem to be at variance with the prevailing view, then they are dismissed as being unrepresentative or biased.

It is therefore worth remembering that one of the aims of a survey should be to capture good, reliable and representative data in order to conduct a scientific investigation or collect up-to-date information. The survey can also help us to ascertain the views of the 'consumers' of a service. Unfortunately, there are all too frequent examples of services being provided that meet the needs of the 'producers' rather than the 'consumers' in fields such as housing and public transport. The fact that the survey is so commonplace may blind us to the idea that letting the public have its voice may be considered quite a radical idea. Indeed, even within the intellectual traditions of the West, the notion that one should actively try to collect information to throw light upon a question rather than to 'armchair-theorize' is a relatively recent phenomenon.

The following is a list of the reasons that people may have, either intentionally or unintentionally, for conducting a survey and readers are invited to check which of the reasons can be seen as legitimate and which as illegitimate.

(a)   Desire to inform oneself with relevant data collected from a representative sample.
(b)   The collection of data that will tend to support one's view, for example over the desirability of a particular policy or course of action.
(c)   The testing of a research hypothesis in a scientific investigation.
(d)   Responding to the pressure to be 'doing something' about a problem by conducting a survey rather than taking some other form of executive action.
(e)   The conduct of a survey in order to bamboozle with a mass of figures, particularly when supported by obscure statistical jargon and analysis.
(f)   As a delaying tactic in order to attempt to buy time or to hope that a problem may either 'go away' or be handed on to one's successor in an organization.
(g)   As a 'pilot study' for a much larger exercise to be conducted later.
(h)   As a training exercise for students and professionals.
(i)   In order to 'market-research' the market for a new product or service.
(j)   As a 'cover' in order to extract a list of names and addresses from the public for later direct selling methods.
(k)   The creation of a 'climate of opinion' which may increase public consciousness over an issue – for example, the desirability or otherwise of a new bypass around one's local town. The same technique may also raise an item higher up the political agenda of issues that need resolution by either central or local government.
(l)   In order to canvass the views of the public before decisions are taken, particularly in the planning sphere, which may affect the lives of many of the inhabitants of an area.

It is evident that this list is not exhaustive and some of the categories undoubtedly overlap with one another. However, it should not be too difficult to spot that (a), (c), (g), (h), (i) and (l) may be regarded as legitimate reasons for a survey whilst (b), (d), (e), (f), (j) and (k) are not.

It is evident that surveys may be conducted for a variety of motives and not all of them are altruistic. For these reasons, those who are thinking of conducting a survey should attempt to clarify the precise objectives in their own minds and to be aware of the fact that survey results are capable of being manipulated or abused unless conducted in a spirit of free scientific enquiry.

THE TYPES OF SOCIAL SURVEY

It is possible to classify the varieties of the social survey in many different ways, e.g. by timescale, methods of data collection employed, ultimate intention of the survey and so on. For present purposes, we shall make a distinction only between two types of survey, as follows.

Descriptive survey

In this, the most common type of survey, the investigator is interested primarily in discovering information or patterns of information. For example, in a survey of student opinion we may wish to determine which party was voted for at the last General Election or how much a week is spent on rent or food. There may well be patterns in the data which the investigator can explore at leisure – for example, do male students vote differently from female students? Does the amount spent upon books depend upon how much grant is received?

The prime focus of such a survey is therefore to gather data which will inform the investigator and the readers of the research report once the results are published. The major types of question asked will be of the *'How many?'* or *'How often?'* variety. Whilst there may well be interesting variations in the data, the prime aim of such a survey is to describe the major statistical features of the data as such rather than to test a scientific hypothesis.

Analytical survey

This type of survey is one that is specifically designed to throw light upon a research hypothesis. It is the type of survey that might be employed by an academic researcher or by a professional who is particularly interested in trying to unravel patterns of causation. For example, a personnel manager may well be interested to discover the factors that lie behind patterns of absences in various departments. Some of the data might be factual (age, sex, department, number of years of service) whilst other data might be more subjective ('perceived levels of stress within the job'). The personnel manager could then proceed to test the hypothesis that factors such as 'perceived stress levels' have much more explanatory power than the other so-called 'objective' factors.

The analytical survey should only be conducted after the researcher is well versed in the relevant literature and has good grounds for exploring particular lines of enquiry. A scientific hypothesis will have to be formulated in which the original concepts that the researcher has in mind (e.g. 'stress') are turned into an 'operational definition' (in this case, the score on a series of questions designed to test stress). It could well be that many interesting findings emerge from an analytical survey but its prime focus is to test possible explanations rather than to describe the data as such.

It is evident that the descriptive and the analytical types of survey should be seen as two ends of a continuum rather than as completely distinct categories. There may be occasions when the investigator is attempting to explore data with no research hypotheses as such in mind (or only hypotheses at a very general level). This might be the stage in which 'facts' are gathered after which the investigator seeks to infer a theory to explain them – the 'inductive' phase of scientific investigation. After a theory has been formulated, the investigator would then seek to draw out from it various hypotheses that would serve as a test of that theory – this is the 'deductive' phase of scientific investigation. However, the rather broad distinction that has been drawn between descriptive and analytic surveys should serve for most purposes.

THE PLANNING AND CONDUCT OF SURVEYS

Let us imagine that you were to ask somebody how they would go about their task if they had never conducted a survey before but were charged with the task of conducting one in a hurry. You might ask them what would be involved and what they would consider to be the major stages of the exercise. The answer might well be 'To ask some questions, get the computer to analyse them and then produce a report.' This answer would not be completely wrong but it does miss out some of the crucial stages. There is also the implication that data collection ('Asking some questions') may be the lengthiest part of the procedure, with the analysis being relatively rapid. However, this assumption is almost certainly wrong. The data collection stage can be relatively short whilst the initial preparatory stages and the subsequent analysis of the data may take very much longer than originally anticipated.

What follows is a list of the stages involved in the planning and execution of the successful survey. This list is brief and readers are recommended to other sources to provide a more systematic rationale of each of the stages. None the less, it does provide a useful checklist if you are in a hurry and need to get reliable results as quickly as possible.

Literature search

Every piece of research should ideally build upon what is already known. This means consulting the storehouse of locked-up learning (the library!) to find out if the proposed survey is really necessary. It could well be that other researchers have recently reported some findings which would make one's own research unnecessary. Even if there is not an exact coincidence of interests, it is often the case that the cost of an additional survey is not justified if another researcher's results can be utilized in some way. This is particularly true for the larger-scale surveys which have a correspondingly higher price tag!

Even if the proposed topic of your research has already been surveyed, there may be good grounds for proceeding with your own plans. The results of a survey that have already been published may be dated or based upon a somewhat different population. Apart from anything else, the process of **replication** (attempting to check on previously published results by asking similar or identical questions) is generally good scientific practice and can add to the credibility and to the interest generated in your own results.

The available literature may well have gaps in it. This then provides an ideal justification for one's own piece of work. But the principal justification for the literature search is the assumption that you wish your own survey to add to a growing body of knowledge. By knowing and acknowledging the contributions of the others who have surveyed similar topics before, you are contributing to the storehouse of knowledge for future workers in the field. The same general principle will still apply to privately commissioned market research. Although previous results may not have been released for publication, they still provide a context into which you can locate your own piece of work.

Choice of data collection methods

The choice of data collection methods is largely determined by the nature of the problem under investigation. We might think of data collection methods as spread out along a continuum. At one end, we would wish to collect data from a large number of people so as to achieve **representativeness**. Administering a questionnaire to a national sample of nurses in order to determine the number of hours worked per week would be an example of this type. At the other end of the continuum, we might wish to study a small number of individuals intensively in order to generate an **insight** into their particular social worlds. For example, the researcher might join a self-help group for single parents as a participant or observer – representativeness would be unimportant compared with the insights that could be gained. And of course, there would be points in-between where we try to achieve the necessary balance by trading off 'representativeness' on the one hand against 'insights' on the other. One way to represent this continuum is as follows.

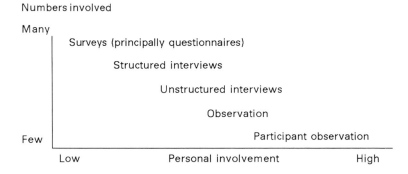

Numbers involved

Many

Surveys (principally questionnaires)

Structured interviews

Unstructured interviews

Observation

Few | Participant observation

Low   Personal involvement   High

Source: Worsley, P. (1977) Introducing Sociology, 2nd edn, Ch.2, Penguin, Harmondsworth.

Many sources on survey design tend to give the impression that you only choose one of the available methods of data collection but this is not so. The most powerful social survey is one that combines the questionnaire method which achieves representativeness, with the insights generated by a case study of selected individuals.

For the remainder of this discussion, we shall assume that readers are interested in collecting data from a reasonably large number of individuals, probably by questionnaire, and intend to process this data statistically.

Choice of sampling frame

Statisticians make a distinction between a **population** (i.e. category of units or events in which we are interested such as 'part-time students', soft drinks sold, cases of arson in a large city) and a **sample**. A sample is a part of the population chosen in such a way so as to be representative of the wider population from which it is drawn. Sometimes it is not necessary to sample if the population is sufficiently small. But we often need to sample because it is not feasible to study the whole population. We can apply a body of statistical theory to the results that we obtain from our sample to indicate the likely range of results we would find if it had been possible to survey the whole of the population.

Before we can draw a sample, we need a **sampling frame**. This is a list which includes at least the members of the population in which we are interested (and may contain others as well). Popular sampling frames are the payroll of an organization, the electoral register or even a telephone directory (readers are left to ponder whether the latter would introduce any biases into the sample which was selected on this basis or not).

The principal types of sample design will be discussed later.

Pilot stage

The concept of a pilot stage is that of a 'trial run' of the survey. If a questionnaire is to be used, it should have been tried out first on a sample other than that for which it is intended. This gives the opportunity to check that any questions asked are unambiguous or that the form does not mislead people unintentionally. For example, the 1991 Census in Great Britain had a series of questions which were designed to exclude students who had a temporary job in the vacations from being regarded as permanently employed. However, the questions were misinterpreted by substantial numbers of people resulting in an over-recording of those in full-time permanent employment. A better piloting of the whole census might have alerted the census designers to the possibility of confusion thus saving months of work and thousands of pounds in extra processing costs.

The pilot stage also gives the opportunity to test out other aspects of the organization of the survey before one is committed to a particular choice of survey design. For example, the data may take longer to transfer into a computer for the analysis than had originally been anticipated.

Data collection stage

Before the actual data collection is undertaken, it is generally extremely important to gain the permission of the relevant people in an organization. For example, one would need the permission of the manager of a firm before engaging in a survey of employees and their supervisors. In the social research literature, such individuals are often known as 'gatekeepers' because, as they control the flow of resources, their co-operation is essential. If the necessary permissions have been granted, then one of the obstacles to a successful survey has been removed (but there may be more). On the other hand, if the necessary permissions have not been sought and obtained, then the investigator runs the risk of having the whole project brought to a premature end by being denied access to the respondents.

Data collection can be directly from respondents, for example by questionnaire or interview, or from documents. If the results of the survey are to be analysed statistically, then careful consideration should be given to the design of the documents which will aid an efficient transfer of data into a computer format. More detailed suggestions are given in Chapter 3.

The importance of getting full and accurate data cannot be overemphasized and for these reasons the **response rate** is particularly important. If a response rate of less than 50% is achieved (and over 70% should be regarded as the acceptable minimum) then whatever results are obtained can be queried ('What about the 50% of people who did not reply?'). There are well-recognized techniques for securing efficient response rates but amongst the most important are the following:

- a covering letter signed by as prestigious a person as possible explaining the aims of the survey and inviting co-operation;
- tangible rewards for the respondents in the nature of either a small gift (e.g. providing a low-cost ball-point pen with which to complete the questionnaire) or a promise to make the results of the survey available to them once the analysis is complete;
- psychological inducements, for example a stamped and addressed envelope of the type in which the stamp has been affixed by hand seems to induce a higher response rate than an official envelope;
- making sure that the questionnaire is of reasonable length and, in particular, is not too long or complicated.

The data input, validation and analysis stage

This is the stage when the data is fed into a computer system and then analysed. Firstly, a **datafile** has to be prepared, usually in the form of numbers that the appropriate software can recognize. It is often helpful at the data input stage to make use of a database such as dBASE III to ease the data entry – in such software, the user can design an input screen which makes the input of large amounts of data particularly easy, especially in the correction of input errors.

If it is important that the data is of the highest quality, which is generally the case, then we need to consider **data validation**. This is a procedure in which the data is entered a second time and the second datafile compared with the first in order to try to eliminate data errors due to mistyped keystrokes. Evidently, if the two files of data do not agree, then the investigator needs to search for the source of the error and eliminate it before producing a datafile which is deemed to be 'error free'. Data validation can trap most but not all errors. If the same error was made in the same place on two separate occasions then an inconsistency will not be 'flagged', nor can data validation make up for the fact that the data might have been badly recorded initially. However, it can help to ensure that errors due to incorrect data entry are minimized.

The data analysis stage consists of using the appropriate software (**TURBOSTATS**, for example) to produce the frequency distributions, cross-tabulations and other statistical analyses that may be required. These terms will be explained further in the later chapters of this book.

The 'writing-up' and 'report-back' stages

Once the analyses have been performed, then the results need to be written up in a format which should have been agreed in advance with the sponsors. For example, it could well be that the statistical tables are printed in full in an appendix whilst relevant extracts are also reproduced in the body of the text and discussed.

When writing up a research report, it is important to bear in mind who the readers of the report are likely to be. If the results are to be incorporated in an academic paper, then it would be permissible to introduce the appropriate technical terminology, for example reporting the results of a significance test. On the other hand, documents written with the general public in mind would have to be written in a different style and with the technical details kept to a bare minimum. Often, the writer is attempting to satisfy several audiences simultaneously and there is no easy answer to the problem. One compromise is to adopt the format of a one- or two-page summary for the 'general public' readers, with the main body of the report written for the sponsors and most of the technical details confined to an appendix for the more technically informed.

Consideration should also be given to a brief document in which the results can be communicated back to the original respondents. This is the researcher fulfilling his/her part of the 'effort bargain'. In return for providing the time for completing the survey, the respondents are provided with a summary of the results of the research upon publication. The dissemination of the results should also be considered. Once the research has been conducted, then one wishes to bring it to the attention of other researchers in the field or other organizations or individuals who would have an interest in the results.

THE PROCESS OF SAMPLING

Earlier, reference was made to a sampling frame being a list which contained the names of those people whom one might contact for a survey. However, even given such a list (e.g. all of those on the payroll of a company) the problem becomes how one selects or draws a sample from such a list. It must be remembered that our aim is to collect data from a sample which is representative of the population from which it is drawn. How, then, do we actually go about this task?

There are two principal methods for the drawing of samples and even more specialized sub-types of sampling method which will not be explored in detail. Rather the two 'families' of sample design will be considered – the **random sample** and the **quota sample**.

The random sample

A random sample is one in which each unit has either the same, or a calculable, chance of being chosen. Thus if we were to sample 50 patients from an intake of 1000 patients, each patient would have a 1 in 20 chance of being selected for the sample. But how do we choose at random? The human brain is not very good at 'thinking randomly' and we need a computer to assist us in generating some tables of random numbers. (As an aside, computers actually generate what are termed 'pseudo-random' numbers which are the results of the repeated application of an algebraic formula which has the properties of producing numbers that **appear** to be random, i.e. there are approximately equal numbers of ones, twos, . . ., nines and so on.) Many calculators also possess a random number generator as well.

If we wished to draw a random sample of 50 patients from a **numbered** list of 1000 patients then we would consult our random number generator from a calculator or a list of random numbers from a statistics textbook and proceed as follows. If our random number generator gives numbers from 0 to 0.999 then our first number that we might generate might be 0.199. We would then select case number 199 as the first case in our sample. If we only had 800 in our population, then we would ignore random numbers from 0.800 upwards and continue generating random numbers until we found one that came within the required range. We would carry on generating random numbers until we had collected a sample of the relevant size.

A problem, though, can arise. What about the case where the **same** random number appears twice – should we select patient number 199 twice? If we wished to sample documentary records then it would be regarded as legitimate to select the same unit twice because this preserves the principle that every unit has the same chance of being selected (called **sampling with replacement**). However, if we are selecting a sample of people for a questionnaire then it would not be very sensible to select the same person twice and in that case we would select another person for our sample, which actually breaks the principle of each person having the **same** chance of being selected. In effect, we are saying that patient number 199 has a 1 in 1000 chance of being selected if they were the first to be drawn and they are, in effect, then 'removed' from the population. So the next person selected has 1 chance in 999 of being selected, that is slightly less than a chance in 1000. This process is known as **sampling without replacement**. Fortunately, statisticians are able to make slight adjustments to their formulae to accommodate this. For the practitioner of a small-scale survey, this should not be a major source of concern.

The advantage of using a system of random numbers is that a body of statistical theory can be applied to the results that we obtain. If we are trying to estimate how much people spend on average each week upon their transport needs, for example, we might obtain an estimate from our sample of £15.00 a week. Once we have some statistical measures from our sample data (specifically the **mean** and the **standard deviation**) then we can engage in a few quite simple calculations that will enable us to make an estimate of the range within which the mean for the whole population, if we were able to determine it, is likely to lie. We can also specify the degree of **confidence** that we place in our estimates. For example, we might be able to state that we are 95% confident that the figure for the transport needs of the entire population will lie within the range of, say, £13–£17 a week. Of course, we cannot be absolutely certain that the mean for the whole population is likely to lie within this range – we may have been unfortunate and picked a sample which spent much more (or less) than the national average on transport. None the less, the body of statistical theory does enable us to use our sample to make some sensible estimates of the values, such as averages, that would be found in the whole population.

The fact that we can make such statements, based on probability, derives from the properties of large numbers of cases which have given rise to the theorems of statistics. This does not guarantee that we actually have selected a representative sample – indeed, by the laws of chance we may select a poor one if we are unlucky. But the body of statistical theory allows us to calculate our chances of getting an unrepresentative sample and increases the confidence that we, and other people, might place in our results.

There are varieties of random sample which avoid the necessity to use random number generators and the like. One very common method is to select, for example, every 20th name on the electoral register, often termed a 'quasi-random' sample. But even here there are pitfalls for the unwary. If we were to select every 20th house in a street in particular parts of our cities, we could arrive at a sample of corner shops. And the practice of choosing every 20th name, for example, does increase the chances of selecting individuals from large families which might introduce other biases.

There are two varieties of random sample that might be mentioned briefly. The first of these is a **stratified** sample. If we know that the proportion of women to men in a particular organization is 60:40, then it would be quite valid to pick 60% of the sample from the women members of the sampling frame with the remaining 40% from the men. The same principle can be applied to age, department and so on. A moment's reflection will reveal that we are still preserving the principle that every person has an approximately equal chance of being selected. The second major variety of random sample is a **multi-stage** sample. If we were to select a national sample of patients, we might first have to construct a sample of Regional Health Authorities, then of hospitals within those authorities, then of wards within those hospitals and finally of patients within the wards.

The disadvantage of the random sample is that we buy statistical precision at a price. Once a person has been selected in a random sample, then no other person will do! If another person is substituted, then the principle of randomness has been abandoned and sources of bias **may** creep into the sample. As a practical illustration, the author once participated in a National Food Survey in which the government interviewed a random sample of the population to collect information about diet and food-buying habits. It was not uncommon when the data was being collected for an individual in the chosen household to say to the interviewer that they were too busy – 'why not go next door to "Mrs Smith", who is a lonely old-age pensioner and who would welcome the chance of a talk even with an interviewer'! Readers are left to draw the appropriate conclusions as to what happens if interviewers were to depart from their selected lists of individuals. However, it can be difficult to explain to members of the general public why they have been selected and the interview has to be conducted with them and them alone and not with the person next door.

The fact that only the named individuals will suffice adds to the costs of collecting the data – when the interviewer calls, the person selected for the sample may be on holiday, in hospital, away on business, working shifts and so on. This then necessitates a repeated visit, several times if necessary, until the interview has been obtained or the case has been abandoned as unreachable. The genuine random sample is therefore a 'Rolls-Royce' in that it gives a degree of precision but at a price. If the results of the survey are not of earth-shattering importance (e.g. what kind of cat food does one buy?) then there may be cheaper alternatives.

The quota sample

If we know in advance that we require a sample of 1000 individuals in order to conduct a public opinion survey, then there are quicker and easier alternatives to the random sample. The **quota** sample works on the basis that we know from existing published statistics the proportions of men and women in the general population as well as their ages, social class distribution and perhaps other characteristics. (Incidentally, the three categories of age, sex and social class are the three most important ways in which market researchers segment the market.) Using these statistics, we can then calculate how many individuals of each sex, age group and social class we need to select for our sample. Once we have constructed the quota table, it is possible to go out into the street and select any individuals that are needed to fill up the 'cells' of our sample – we know that it will contain all of the correct proportions because we have constructed it in that particular way. The figure on page 14 illustrates this point.

An example of a quota sample for the adult population

The data illustrated on page 14 has been calculated from figures published in *Social Trends* and should be regarded as approximate. *Social Trends* is published annually by HMSO and is often regarded as a 'bible' by those requiring rapid access to official statistics in the social sphere. *Social Trends* is well worth consulting if only for a demonstration of the many different ways in which it is possible to illustrate data graphically.

Each cell is calculated as follows. We know that we need 210 individuals in their 20s and, of these, we also know that we need in total

Social class	Women					Men					
	I	II	III	IV	V	I	II	III	IV	V	
20–29	1	23	49	25	10	6	23	49	17	7	210
30–39											200
40–49											162
50–59											168
60–69											146
70–79											114
	5	109	235	120	45	28	109	235	83	31	1000
			514					486			

109 social class II women. As there are 1000 in the entire sample, then the number of social class II women in their 20s that we need is 109 × 210/1000 which is 22.9 (or 23 to the nearest whole number). Each other cell is worked out in a similar way.

Interviewers are then asked to approach any individuals in the chosen interview location who look as though they are women, in their 20s and also in social class II and, if so, they can then be approached to participate in the sample. In practice, interviewers will be given a selection of cases or their own individual table which may be a scaled-down version of the entire 'master table'. Readers may well have experienced being 'looked over' by an interviewer who is consulting his/her clipboard trying to assess whether or not they seem likely to fall into the allocated quota.

The quota sample seems initially complicated but is actually fairly quick to design and also swift to administer – **any** individuals who 'fit' into the cells will do and hence interviewers will often work in busy shopping centres where the choice of interviewees is greatest. But, as with the random sample, there are hidden dangers. Imagine the following scenario. It is a cold November morning and it is raining. You need one case to fulfil your quota (e.g. the one social class II woman in her 20s). You are paid by your results, not the amount of time that you spend. As with the board game 'Scrabble' the first few cases are easy but then it becomes increasingly difficult to find the one remaining case. After approaching 50 young women in their 20s and who appear to be social class II, you find somebody who is a woman, social class II but who is 30 years old. What are you tempted to do?

It is well known that even well-trained and well-paid interviewers will 'bend' their results in order to fulfil their quota. What does this do for the representativeness of the data? Suddenly, some of the advantages of speed and therefore cheapness associated with the quota sample seem to be evaporating. There are also other disadvantages as well. Locating oneself in a busy shopping mall in a large city will bias the data towards those who shop/work in the centre of a large city and systematically under-record the 'transport poor' who find access to the city more difficult. Also the time at which sampling is conducted is important. One will often get a different clientele in public places according to both the day of the week and the time of day and unless these are varied, then again the quota may well be skewed.

The disadvantages of quota sampling stem mainly from the fact that there is not a body of statistical theory that we can apply to the results to estimate what the 'true' results are in the general population. It is true that we may have constructed a sample that matches that of the general population but there may be important biases in the data of which we are unaware, particularly if the sampling takes place in a public place.

However, market researchers claim convincingly that because a quota sample is fairly cheap to collect, then it is possible to process a much larger sample and, other things being equal, a large sample will be a better predictor of trends in the population than a smaller one. Also, there are conditions, particularly in the case of opinion polls conducted at election time, when the public mood is very volatile and it is necessary to poll quickly and often – a random sample cannot be collected and published within the available timescale. As with the choice of methods, so the choice of sampling technique often depends upon the nature of the problem which is being researched.

The choice of sample size is another important consideration. Statistical textbooks will give the precise formulae for indicating the degree of precision that can be gained when increasing the sample size. The important rule to remember is that it is the **absolute size** of the sample rather than the proportion that the sample bears to the population which is the critical factor. For a sample of the whole population, market researchers and opinion pollsters typically use a sample of about 1500 individuals. Doubling this sample size to 3000 might only give an increase in precision of 1% or 2% and probably could not be justified in terms of cost.

A final consideration, well illustrated in the quota sample table above, is that the size of the sample may well be dictated by the size of the smallest cell that you wish to analyse statistically. In this case, if you recall, we have only one social class II woman in her 20s (there are not many in the whole population). In a case like this, we would need to combine categories and we generally need a cell size (or a combined cell size) of around 30 before we are in a position to work out meaningful percentages. The size of the smallest cell may seem to be a backwards way of working out the sample size but it is sensible when you consider the overall objectives of the survey. Once a particular sample size has been achieved, then considerations of cost often dictate the upper sample size. Increasing the sample size, particularly once the sample size is sufficiently large, may have only a marginal impact on the ability of the sample to estimate the values to be found in the whole population.

The processes and perils of research 2

FORMULATING THE RESEARCH PROBLEM

When we start to undertake some research, we might imagine that we have a fairly clear idea of the nature of the problem that we intend to pursue in our investigation. As the time approaches to make more concrete plans, however, it can become surprisingly difficult to translate our general objectives into the types of issues upon which we can actually gather meaningful data. A practical illustration may make this clear. Let us imagine that we wish to conduct a 'customer satisfaction' survey to discover whether the users of a leisure centre are satisfied with the facilities provided. When we think about what constitutes a 'customer', we might immediately think of a sample of the individuals who come through the doors of our leisure centre in a typical week. But a moment's reflection may indicate that we need to be thinking about not only actual customers but also potential customers. It is possible that the leisure centre is only attracting a particular **type** of customer, for other groups may have sampled the facilities on one occasion only and found things so unattractive that they said to themselves 'Never again!' So focusing on the actual customers rather than the potential customers may give us a misleading impression as the sample is self-selecting. Again, the problem of what constitutes 'satisfaction' may be difficult to define. Do we mean the absence of 'dissatisfaction' or do we mean the expression of more positive attitudes? Trying to get an overall measure of satisfaction may, in turn, prove very difficult. A typical response might be that 'I find the facilities attractive but the prices are higher than I can generally afford.' In these circumstances, we need to clarify our precise objectives (e.g. the nature of our 'market', what we mean by 'satisfaction') to make our survey more focused.

CONCEPTS AND INDICATORS

We have just alluded to a very common problem in the whole of the research process when we were trying to define how we measure 'customer satisfaction'. In the language of the social researcher, we wish to make a distinction between the following:

Concepts – often abstract terms, for example 'satisfaction', 'health', 'highly educated'.

Indicators – a measurement which we are able to make, or gather, which we feel can 'stand for' the concept under discussion. So some indicators of health might be medicines bought, visits made to medical practitioners, days of sick leave taken and so on. Indicators of 'customer satisfaction' might be frequency of visits, amount of money spent or even scoring highly on the different components of a 'customer satisfaction' questionnaire.

Operational definitions – may be the expression of concepts in terms of some indicators – for example, the concept of 'highly educated' could be operationally defined as 'having passed degree or degree-level type of examinations'.

We may be left with a nagging doubt that the 'indicators' that we have chosen are very imperfect measures of the underlying phenomenon that we are trying to investigate. Can we be sure that if the customers of our leisure centre make frequent return trips that they are really satisfied with the facilities on offer (as the facilities could be bad but the alternatives could be even worse, or even non-existent)? Do we really measure 'satisfaction' by the answers that may be ticked on a questionnaire? The social researcher has to live with these worries. Being aware that one's indicators may be, at best, imperfect may give the encouragement needed to seek more sensitive and accurate indicators. The investigator needs to be aware that indicators cannot always be taken at face value (e.g. days of absence through sickness may be an indicator of industrial conflict rather than sickness *per se*). Some concepts may need a variety of indicators which, when carefully combined, can explore the multi-dimensional nature of the concept under investigation.

It is also important that the indicators that we choose exhibit the properties of being:

reliable – repeated measures will give similar results when conducted on different occasions;
valid – the indicator is a good measure of the underlying concept.

THE VARIETIES OF RESEARCH DESIGN

The classical experimental method is often taken as the starting point for an examination of the logic underlying a particular investigation, even though the occasions upon which it can be utilized are quite rare. It is assumed that we have a random sample equally divided into the 'Experimental group' (who will be exposed to a 'stimulus') whilst another group, alike in practically all respects save that they have **not** been exposed to the stimulus, form a 'Control group'. The assumption is that any changes which we observe in the 'Experimental group' following the stimulus which are not observable in the 'Control' group can only have come about because of the stimulus they have received. For example, an 'Experimental group' shown a film about the effects of lung cancer may have altered their smoking habits whilst the 'Control group's' smoking habits are unchanged.

This is summarized in the following diagram.

Classical model of experimental design

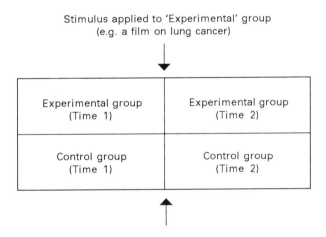

The full classical experimental model, whilst not perfect, is an attempt to ascertain precisely patterns of causal influences. It is therefore used in the analytical rather than the purely descriptive survey. However, circumstances often dictate the need for a variation of the full classical pattern, often because they are beyond the investigator's control. Some common variations are discussed below.

Before and after

For example, smokers' habits were recorded **before** viewing the film and again **after** viewing the film.

Experimental group (Time 1)	Experimental group (Time 2)

The problem here is that we lose the opportunity of a control group. Any changes that we observe could have happened anyway (as part of a general cultural change) and we cannot be certain that the film was responsible for the change in smoking patterns.

Quasi-panel design

For example, smokers' habits were recorded **before** viewing a film and those of a different group recorded **after** the viewing of the film.

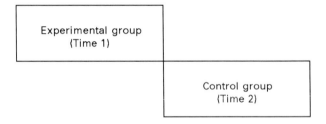

Here we are attempting to measure changes but not necessarily to ascribe causes as the 'after' group is an entirely different sample. This is a model used, for example, by BBC Audience Research. We can record the changes but find it difficult to ascribe causes as whatever changes we observe could be because the composition of the groups has changed rather than the stimulus (the content of the film in this case) is having an effect.

Cross-sectional design

For example, smokers and non-smokers had previously been shown a film and the results are now being evaluated.

This kind of research design is quite common where the researcher only has access to the subjects of the investigation **after** the application of a stimulus. For example, an advertising campaign might already have

```
┌─────────────────────────────┐
│                             │
│     Experimental group      │
│         (Time 2)            │
│                             │
├─────────────────────────────┤
│                             │
│       Control group         │
│         (Time 2)            │
│                             │
└─────────────────────────────┘
```

taken place and we are trying to weigh the opinions of those who had seen the advertisement against those who had not. In a case like this, the investigator tries to supply the 'missing boxes' mentally or may ask the subjects to attempt to recall their views before they had seen the advertisement in question.

Case-study design

For example, smokers are asked their views on the risks involved.

```
┌─────────────────────────────┐
│                             │
│     Experimental group      │
│         (Time 1)            │
│                             │
└─────────────────────────────┘
```

Here a single group is studied intensively. The intention of a survey of this type is not so much to ascertain 'causes' but rather to gather data in depth. Many opinion and attitude surveys are of this type – we would need to design further surveys if we wish to unravel the causal influences which may be at work.

In all of these designs, it is important to stress that the investigator is adapting some of the techniques known to work well 'in the laboratory' in order to analyse complex human behaviour patterns. In the case of the variations in the full classical experimental design, the investigator is forced to 'fill in the missing boxes' either mentally or by other means. Under these circumstances, the investigator can be less than certain that the behaviour pattern observed is only due to the 'stimulus' that might have triggered the changes and not due to the operation of other factors. There is also debate about whether this mode of investigation is suitable, in any case, for the investigation of complex behaviour patterns. If we are interested in 'buyer behaviour', for example, can we really be convinced that we have captured the 'true' reasons for a particular pattern of purchase within the scope of our investigation? However, even with these reservations, the investigator is in a position to draw **tentative** conclusions regarding causal influences if the study has shown some elements of careful design. In the example quoted above, for example, we cannot be absolutely convinced that the impact of a film is a major, or even the only, cause of a modification in smokers' behaviour patterns. But with the evidence of experimental and control groups in the 'cross-sectional design' study, we are in a stronger position to attempt to ascertain causal influences than would otherwise be the case.

PRACTICAL ISSUES IN SURVEY ORGANIZATION

After examining some of the issues that are fundamental to the design of a survey, we now turn our attention to some practical, but often neglected, issues in survey organization.

Negotiating access and securing co-operation

Once we have a survey design in mind, the next problem becomes whether or not it is feasible to make contact with the groups that we wish to investigate. If the subjects of the proposed investigation are at one physical site (e.g. the employees of a company) then our problems may be eased but not eliminated. There may well be patterns of shift or holiday working that can make actual contact difficult, not to mention the fact that people often have stressful full-time jobs to do in which a survey may come low down on their list of priorities. If the subjects are physically dispersed, we then have to make pragmatic decisions about whether or not interviewers have to be trained and despatched in order to gather the necessary data or whether we will have to rely upon a mailed questionnaire.

As has already been mentioned in Chapter 1, the investigator has to ensure that he/she has the full co-operation of the relevant managers in an organization before the investigation can proceed. This will generally entail sending a detailed letter of explanation concerning the objectives and scope of the intended survey together with a sample of the questionnaire to be used (if any) and the use to which the results are to be put. Many managers get understandably nervous if they feel that sensitive information is to be uncovered or if they feel that they will bear the consequences for any adverse reactions that the survey may generate. It is therefore the responsibility of the investigator to be prepared to spend a considerable amount of time in briefing the relevant manager(s) and inviting their co-operation. Needless to say, the issue of confidentiality and non-identification of personnel or locations has to be stressed. Without at least the tacit co-operation of the key managerial personnel involved, the survey as a whole could well be abortive. Even getting the co-operation of senior management does not ensure that the 'first-line supervisors' who may themselves be responsible for the day-to-day handling of the questionnaires are fully briefed or informed. Under these circumstances, the investigator is well advised to have a 'briefing document' prepared which explains succinctly but carefully why and how the survey is being conducted. If this briefing document can be reproduced on headed notepaper to authenticate its status and be signed by as prestigious a person as possible, then so much the better.

The necessity of negotiating access and securing the co-operation of relevant personnel is hard to overemphasize. The investigator has to realize that this can be a sensitive area and considerable time and effort may have to be invested in this stage of the investigation before it is even certain that the investigation itself can proceed. It is often a good idea to promise (and keep the promise!) to make the results of the investigation available as a *quid pro quo* for the supervisory effort that may be involved. Just because a senior manager may have given approval to the venture and be fully informed does not guarantee that the same reaction is to be found in other parts of the organization. The investigator may have to explain the points of the investigation several times over to other managerial staff and/or supervisors in order to gain their co-operation.

There are certain kinds of research, particularly in the health and medical fields, where questions of ethics arise. In cases like this, approval has to be sought from the local medical ethical committee, particularly in cases where direct contact with patients is sought. Take the advice of those who are knowledgeable and well informed about the local position and be aware of the fact that research which may be viewed as trivial could clutter up the field for more serious investigators.

The key to much of the discussion above is efficient communication. The investigator cannot take it for granted, however, that if he/she has initiated the communication process (prepared a briefing document, had an interview with the relevant managerial and/or technical staff) that the content of the communication has been internalized. It is a common failing of all organizations that the lower levels complain that they have not received the communication (or realize the implications of the communication) from those in senior levels. The investigator has to ensure that all relevant staff have been communicated with regarding the aims and intentions of the proposed investigation and their co-operation secured.

Negotiating access to the respondents of a survey is a necessary first step but this, by itself, does not ensure that one can get the data that is required. Some ingenuity in the use of psychological inducements may be required to persuade busy personnel that they should co-operate in an investigation. It could well be that a group has been 'oversurveyed' in the past and a certain cynicism greets the unhappy researcher who is unaware of this fact. In the fields of market research, it is commonplace for a low-cost article to be offered as a recompense for the time and trouble involved (a pen often being a good choice). The aim at all times must be to secure the capture of the required volumes of 'high-quality' data which often means, in practice, securing the return of as many questionnaires as possible which have been completed conscientiously.

Budgeting a survey

It is a truism to say that 'surveys take time' and that 'surveys cost money' but this practical aspect of survey organization is very often ignored. The investigator would be well advised to make a 'time-line', that is a timescale that encompasses all of the major components of the survey. An example, in outline only, is shown below:

| I---------I-----------------I------------I------------------I----------I |
| 2 weeks | 4 weeks | 3 weeks | 4 weeks | 2 weeks |
| Literature search | Securing access | Data collection | Data input, validation analysis | Writing up |

Notice that, in this example, the data collection period is short compared with the input, validation and analysis stage. The literature search could well take considerably longer if one is starting *ab initio* and no allowance has been made for a pilot study. Obviously, the investigator should draw his/her own 'time budget' taking into account the size and complexity of the intended survey, not neglecting to build in some extra leeway for unforeseen difficulties in collecting or analysing the data.

Budgeting a survey in monetary terms has to take into account the following items:

• salaries and fees (of interviewers who may have to be trained and then paid by the hour);

- travel costs;
- typing and clerical costs;
- reprography (e.g. photocopying) of questionnaire, which can be a considerable cost;
- postage costs (both outward and return);
- telephone costs;
- costs of producing the final report (and in what number).

Even a small survey may turn out to be quite a lot more expensive than originally envisaged. It cannot be assumed that organizations will turn a blind eye to the often quite substantial costs involved in photocopying several hundred copies of a questionnaire which runs to several pages.

Both the 'time' and the 'cost' budgeting of a survey should evidently be conducted very early in the design stage of the survey. Sponsors are then aware of the likely financial consequences of approving a decision to survey and investigators are in a position to ensure that the likely results will be commensurate with the effort, time and costs that are involved.

SOME COMMON PROBLEMS IN THE CONDUCT OF SURVEYS

Complexity

If the investigator is relatively inexperienced, it is easy to make the survey more complex than it needs to be for the task in hand. In particular, there is often a great danger of 'asking questions for the sake of it'. Armed with a great volume of data, the investigator may then discard some of it at the analysis stage which makes collecting it in the first place rather pointless. A good rule of thumb is to make the number of questions commensurate with the likely number of respondents. If data is only going to be collected from a sample of 50 customers, for example, then there are not going to be enough cases to analyse the data meaningfully with respect to age, sex and any other categories. The investigator needs to bear in mind at all times what the overall dimensions of the analysis are going to look like in terms of frequency distributions and contingency tables. If the initial sample numbers are small, then there is no point in having a variable such as age divided into eight or ten bands (20–29, 30–39, etc.) as the numbers in each band will be too small to make any meaningful statistical generalizations.

The warning about complexity applies not only to the number of categories into which the data is divided but also to the form in which the data is itself collected. The investigator needs to bear in mind that the data should be in a simple numerical form and that multiple choices allowed in one 'column' of data can make the subsequent analysis much more difficult. Here again, a good rule of thumb is to avoid situations in which multiple answers can be 'ticked' and to try to collect the data in a format such that only one response is permitted to a question.

Quantifiable v. non-quantifiable data

Despite the fact that this book is devoted to the computerized analysis of survey data, it has to be recognized that there are some problems which the human brain is much better equipped to handle than a computer. The prime example here is the 'open-ended' question in which the interviewees are left to speak for themselves. Here, by definition, the data is in a non-quantified form and the investigator will need to decide how the subsequent material is to be handled. It may be a rich source of quotes to illustrate some of the themes of the subsequent analysis. Or the responses may indicate lines of enquiry or matters of concern to be pursued at a later date.

The fact that the data is in a non-quantified form does not mean, however, that it is intrinsically non-quantifiable. The researcher can peruse the data to see what categories or themes suggest themselves and then go back and re-analyse the data in terms of these 'emergent' categories. However, this process is time consuming and calls for a degree of judgement and skill on the part of the investigator. One should not avoid open-ended questions because of these difficulties but rather be aware of the uses to which they can be put and the ways in which they need to be analysed.

Recording data

The problems of recording data in the case of a mailed questionnaire or an administered interview schedule should not pose any particular difficulties providing that the questions are unambiguous and have been pre-tested in a pilot procedure. In the case of interview data, a decision has to be taken whether to record the data in a series of interview notes or whether to tape-record (or even video-record) it.

At first sight, it might seem sensible to tape-record an interview – at least one has a complete record of what was said which can then be 'dissected' in detail. However, the presence of a tape recorder can inhibit the free flow of information and may make the interviewee feel ill at ease and hesitant. What appears to be a good 'technical fix' to the problem of recording the data has hidden problems for the unwary.

The most immediate problem is that the tape has to be transcribed in order to produce a 'hard copy' (i.e. printed copy) of what was said. The cost and effort involved in the use of skilled audio-typists to produce such 'hard copy' can be considerable and very time consuming. Getting the 'hard copy' or tape transcripts is only the first stage of the exercise because the mass of data then has to be analysed with the same problems that are witnessed in the analysis of open-ended questions.

In the author's experience it is good practice for interviewers to transcribe their own data, preferably within hours of the original interview being conducted. This will obviously involve playing sections of the tape over and over again and transcribing sentence by sentence. The advantage to be gained by this seemingly tedious procedure is that if the transcription takes place within hours of the interview, then the interviewer can remember or reconstruct mumbled or incoherent responses in a way that an audio-typist cannot hope to emulate. In addition, the researcher is also in a position to incorporate his/her own field notes into the transcript (e.g. 'Interviewee seemed distraught at answering this question') thereby adding to the 'richness' of the data collected.

A tape-recorded interview may seem to be the answer to some of the problems involved in getting accurately recorded responses but the investigator needs to be aware of the subsequent problems of analysis and to undertake the procedure with fully open eyes! A good set of 'interview notes' may well prove to be a better solution to the problem of recording the data.

Ensuring representativeness

A final point to be borne in mind at all times is that the investigator is anxious to get representative data. This problem has to be handled at all stages of the investigation but with the critical stages being:

(a)   the selection of the initial sample;
(b)   the pattern of responses from those who actually reply.

If the prime intention of the survey is to secure the type of quantitative analysis in which we say that 'x% of those interviewed indicate y% level of satisfaction' then we have to make every effort to ensure that no systematic biases are built into our sample. As we have already seen, a quota sample may be particularly prone to picking up an 'unrepresentative' sample and even altering locations and times of the data collection may not solve this problem. Also the pattern of non-response to a mailed questionnaire should be another area of concern. If the researcher keeps a careful record of those to whom the questionnaire has been sent and those who reply, usually with the aid of a coding number, then it should be possible to discern trends of non-response. Under these circumstances, efforts can be redoubled to reach the original non-respondents under a 'chasing' or 'reminder' procedure. The extent to which one can effectively chase is limited, one or two reminders probably being the maximum, but in cases like these an extra copy of the questionnaire should always be included (on the assumption that the first one has been thrown away or mislaid). A carefully worded letter emphasizing how important it is to receive back the completed questionnaire can also be sent but the investigator has to be careful to cajole (and not to appear to bully or threaten) potential respondents in order to secure its return.

Using a questionnaire $\quad$ 3

THE CHOICE OF THE QUESTIONNAIRE METHOD

If we decide to collect data for the purposes of our survey, we have a choice whether to collect data from existing documents or from people (or both). We might collect data from payroll records, for example, to ascertain whether salary appears to vary by department. Or we could study the amount of column inches in newspapers devoted to 'soaps' or to foreign affairs.

The information that we collect from individuals may be simple (ticking a box to indicate gender or an age category) or complex (feeling states after the death of a loved one or the ending of a relationship). In general terms, we would use a *questionnaire* to elicit the simple types of information whilst the more complex data would need to be collected in an **interview**. There are intermediate forms of data collection (the **structured interview** or **administered questionnaire**) in which an interviewer is on hand to record the data, generally in simple categories. However, the interviewer will be able to elaborate or explain the questions if the interviewee is unsure how to respond.

The questionnaire and the structured interview are still the most popular forms of collecting data. This is no doubt because they are cheap and can generate meaningful information in the form of tables of statistics reasonably quickly. The rest of this book will concentrate on the questionnaire, particularly when the researcher wants to provide a statistical analysis of the data. However, this is not to deny the validity and indeed the desirability of other forms of data when the nature of the research problem demands it.

The questionnaire has had its critics, and not without reason. These criticisms range from the philosophical (whether we can adequately represent people's motives and intentions from their answers to questions) to the technical (the results can be made to say what one wants them to say).

Some of the criticisms, and responses to them, are noted below.

(a)   'Questionnaires merely represent marks on a piece of paper, not considered responses'

- This is undoubtedly true on many occasions. The researcher cannot distinguish between those responses that are the result of a considered and conscientious approach to the questions and those that are completed rapidly without any attention or thought.
- If the intention of the survey is made sufficiently clear and the respondent is motivated to answer the questions clearly and thoughtfully (e.g. by knowing that they may ultimately receive a copy of the results) then the danger may be minimized but not eliminated.

(b)   'It is possible to construct a questionnaire to get the results you want'

- This is indeed possible if the questions are written in such a way that they 'invite' an answer, if the relevant questions are not asked or if the results of all the questions are not displayed.
- If the questionnaire is reproduced **in full** together with the results of the analysis of those questions in the form of **frequency distributions**, then the reader can assess whether the questionnaire was of sufficient quality for the results to be taken seriously.

(c)   'People have to reply to questions in categories that might not reflect their true opinions'

- This is a standard criticism of the 'forced choice' type of question. For example, in a survey of opinions regarding Britain's membership of the EC a question might be difficult to answer if you are in favour **politically** of Britain's membership but feel that in **economic terms** it has been a disaster.
- The solution to this ever-present problem is for the designer to be careful not to present the respondent with questions to which the replies might be oversimplistic (as in the example above). Although they are more difficult to analyse, thought should be given to presenting the respondent with the occasional 'open' rather than 'forced choice' questions which

allow the respondent to answer in words of his/her own, when necessary. Such 'open' questions then have to be examined by the researcher to ascertain which categories 'emerge' from the data. The responses can then be 'coded' in much the same way as 'forced choice' questions but into the categories that have emerged from the analysis.

(d)   'The response rate might be very low'

- If the response rate is very low and one suspects that the pattern of 'unreturned' questionnaires may differ significantly from those 'already' returned, then this criticism is very telling.
- The greatest care should be taken to maximize response by the use of incentives both material and symbolic. Subsequent 'chasing' of those who had not initially replied may reveal some of the reasons for the initial non-response and also whether their profile matches those of the questionnaires originally received. A minimum return rate of 70% should be regarded as an acceptable minimum.

Despite these very real criticisms of the questionnaire method, one has to be careful not to 'throw out the baby with the bath water'. Indeed, the questionnaire may be the only way of ensuring that one's survey achieves the required level of **representativeness** whilst acknowledging that it may be at its most powerful when combined with other survey methods. A detailed case study or the results of a few in-depth interviews supplementing the more general data provided by questionnaire can increase the effectiveness of the overall survey enormously.

TYPES OF VARIABLES

Before we start an examination of how to construct and administer a questionnaire, it would be useful to imagine what we feel our results might eventually look like. In this way, we can construct a questionnaire that is easy to analyse and presents the results clearly.

Statisticians make a distinction between the following types of variables.

Nominal or categorical variables

These are variables that put responses into 'boxes' or categories. The best known examples are sex, marital status, smoker or non-smoker and so on. These may well be coded for subsequent analysis in a numerical way, e.g. Female as a (1) and Male as a (2). However, it is important to recognize that the numbers are themselves essentially meaningless and are only a way of distinguishing one category from another.

Ordinal variables

These are very similar to nominal variables except that it is possible to put responses into an assumed order. The best known example is social class in which it is presumed that social class I has more prestige and/or remuneration than social class III or social class V.

Continuous variables

These are variables that can represent one point along a continuous (and theoretically infinite) scale. The best known examples would include one's height, weight or income. These can generally be measured fairly precisely, whereas sex, for example, can only take one of two values.

These distinctions are often explained in the early chapters of statistics textbooks but their true significance does not become plain until one starts to design a questionnaire. By appreciating the distinction right at the start, we can then design our questions properly.

QUESTIONNAIRE ANALYSIS AS AN AID TO DESIGN

If we have some indication of what our final analysis is going to look like, then this aids us enormously in the design of the questionnaire. It helps to ensure that we frame our questions in a way that lends itself to the subsequent processing. At the same time, it helps us to guard against unnecessary questions, for what is the point of collecting data if it is never going to be analysed?

Anticipating somewhat the more detailed explanations to be found in later chapters, let us first have a look at the most common types of statistical treatment of questionnaires. For this purpose, **nominal** and **ordinal** variables will be regarded as one type of variable and **continuous** variables as another. When we wish to present the results of our survey, it is important that we choose the right kind of statistics and methods of presentations appropriate to the types of variables we have employed.

For example, here we are examining the type of newspaper that people read:

PAPER Newspaper read   File: MYSURVEY.TXT

Value Label	Value	Frequency	Percent	Valid Percent	Cum Percent
None	1	40	13.3	15.4	15.4
Quality	2	30	10.0	11.5	26.9
Middle-brow	3	47	15.7	18.1	45.0
Tabloid	4	24	8.0	9.2	54.2
Evening	5	34	11.3	13.1	67.3
Sunday	6	20	6.7	7.7	75.0
Specialist Mag.	7	31	10.3	11.9	86.9
Music Magazine	8	33	11.0	12.7	99.6
Academic Journal	9	1	0.3	0.4	100.0
	0	40	13.3	MISSING	
		------------	------------	------------	
TOTAL		300	100.0	100.0	

```
              None  ███████  40
           Quality  █████  30
       Middle-brow  ████████  47
           Tabloid  ████  24
           Evening  ██████  34
            Sunday  ███  20
    Specialist Mag. ██████  31
    Music Magazine  ██████  33
   Academic Journal ▪ 1
```

Valid Cases   260   Missing Cases   40

In this (hypothetical) survey, people have been presented with a list of different types of newspapers and asked which one of them they read most often in the last week. The respondents had to choose one of nine categories (ranging from 1–None to 9–Academic journal) whilst the value of 0 was reserved for those who did not answer this question at all.

The data is gathered at the nominal level and what the results reveal is a **frequency distribution**. We can tell the total numbers who have replied to each question. Moreover, we can tell the percentage that this represents of the total (Percent) and the percentage that this represents of those who replied to the question (Valid percent). Finally, we have a cumulative distribution in which the percentages are cumulatively added up, each category incorporating the one that went before it, until they add up to 100%. To illustrate the data, we have a small **bar chart** which represents these results graphically. We might also have utilized a **pie chart** if we have access to the appropriate software.

This is the most common type of analysis performed in a questionnaire. The data is measured at the nominal (categorical) level and the results are presented in the form of a frequency distribution. There are many cases where, if we were concerned solely with information gathering, this type of analysis would be entirely sufficient for our purposes.

In the preceding example, we were examining **one** variable – newspaper readership. To reveal patterns in our survey, we very often examine **two** variables at the same time. We do this by forming what is termed a **contingency table** and an example is shown next.

Cross tabulation of CLASS By SEX		Social Class Sex of Individual		File: MYSURVEY.TXT
SEX > **CLASS**		**Male** 1	**Female** 2	**ROW TOTAL**
Professional	1	24	18	42
Intermediate	2	17	5	22
Skilled Manual	3	15	22	37
Semi-skilled Manual	4	27	26	53
Unskilled Manual	5	33	33	66
Pensioners	6	4	22	26
Not classified	7	26	12	38
TOTAL		146 51.4%	138 48.6%	284 100.0%

Valid cases = 284   Missing = 16

In this example, we are interested to see how the sample breaks down in terms of its sex and social class composition. The data is presented in the barest categories at this stage, but we shall see eventually how we can elaborate this table with the appropriate percentages that fall into each cell.

The variables so far have been of the **categorical** or **nominal** type – that is, we have seen how many there are of each sex, each social class or read a particular newspaper. If we wish to examine the other principal category of variable – **continuous variables** – then we are going to have to make use of some more sophisticated statistics. An example of 'Anticipated salary' statistics is shown next.

File: SALARIES.TXT	SALARIES
Measures of central tendency	
Mean	11 023.500
Median	11 000.000
Mode	7 100.000
Measures of dispersion	
Minimum	7 000.000
Maximum	15 000.000
Range	8 000.000
First quartile	8 550.000
Third quartile	13 275.000
Semi-interquartile range	4 725.000
Variance	6 349 397.750
Standard deviation (population)	2 519.801
Standard deviation (sample)	2 526.124
Standard error of the mean	178.624
Numbers of Cases	
N	200
Missing values	0

Many of these statistical terms may seem strange to you but do not worry about this at this stage. **Measures of central tendency** are different ways of measuring an **average** or one value that can somehow be said to represent the rest, whilst **measures of dispersion** are indications of whether the data is well spread out or bunched together.

Many, but not all, surveys can be analysed with the three tools presented here – the frequency distribution, the contingency table and the descriptive statistics. By appreciating at the design stage how the results will appear in your final research report, you will be in a position to design a much better questionnaire.

QUESTIONNAIRE CONSTRUCTION

There are several principles to be followed here, many of them a matter of common sense.

(a) *Do not make the questionnaire too long or complicated.* Long questionnaires tend not to get returned or else try the motivation of the respondent. Aim for a questionnaire which at the most takes 15 minutes if it is to be filled in by the respondent unaided, which is typically so in the case of a mailed questionnaire.

(b) *Make the data easy to 'transfer' from the questionnaire document to the computer.* The choices should be clearly represented with numbers (not letters) to circle or boxes to tick. Data transfer is often made easier if there is a *'For office use only'* column on the right-hand side of the form where numbers may be entered by the investigator.

(c) *Ensure that the instructions for 'navigating' the form are clear.* Not all questions apply to all people. Therefore it may be necessary to employ what is called a 'filter question' and then use the answers to this question to direct people to the appropriate sections of the form.

(d) *Select the 'open' and 'closed' formats with care.* The 'open format' is a question of the following type:

Would you like to explain, in a sentence or so of your own words, your views about Britain's membership of the European Community?

....

....

....

In this type of format, the respondent is not being 'forced into a box' and is free to express himself/herself more freely. But questions of this type leave a lot of work for the subsequent analysis. The investigator will have to read all of the replies and then perhaps summarize them briefly in a large table. Then it will be necessary to see what categories emerge from the data – for example, what is the proportion of negative, neutral and positive responses? How often are economic themes mentioned, political themes or a mixture? It is evident that the researcher has to keep a fairly open mind and then has to synthesize the data that emerges into a number of categories which can then be analysed as though they were the answers to a forced choice question. Although questions of this type are useful they should be used sparingly and perhaps only towards the end of the questionnaire itself.

The 'closed format' or 'forced choice' question asks the respondent to select one of a number of alternatives. This makes the questionnaire easy to code but the interviewee has no choice other than to select one of the alternatives offered.

Sample questionnaire fragment

A small portion of a hypothetical public opinion questionnaire is reproduced next.

ATTITUDES TO SMOKING Questionnaire		
	Please put a tick [✔] in one box **only**	*Office use only*
Q1.	What is your opinion about the banning of smoking in all public places? Are you: (1) In favour [ ] (2) Neutral [ ] (3) Opposed [ ]	BANNING
	If you have ticked (1) In favour then ANSWER QUESTION 2 Otherwise, go straight to QUESTION 3	
Q2.	If you are in favour of banning smoking in public places, are you a smoker yourself: (1) Yes [ ] (2) No [ ]	PUBLIC
Q3.	When it is said that smoking damages your health, do you think that this is: (1) Very likely [ ] (2) Quite likely [ ] (3) Rather unlikely [ ] (4) Not at all likely [ ]	HEALTH

There are several features to note about this fragment of questionnaire.

• Notice the 'forced choice' questions. Respondents have been given specific instructions at the start of the questionnaire to tick one box ONLY.

- There is an example here of a 'filter' question in that only those who declare themselves in favour of banning smoking in public places are invited to reply to Question 2, whilst those not in favour are directed to Question 3.
- The right-hand column is labelled 'Office use only' and the column contains a variable name of eight characters or less which is to be used for the subsequent computer analysis as well as a box for recording the answer to the question. Notice that this is on the right-hand side of the form. If you were going to have questions on both sides of the paper, to save paper and cost, then the coding column would need to go on the left-hand side on the back sheet. Then, to preserve confidentiality and excessive paper handling, the coding 'strips' can be cut off from the rest of the document and passed on for computer input. (This practical hint is useful if the numbers involved are likely to be very large – in excess of several hundred, for example.)
- Question 3 is an example of a question designed to measure the intensity of an attitude. The categories have been deliberately designed to exclude 'neutral' or 'Do not know' answers and are therefore intended to nudge respondents into either a positive or a negative response. There is a good reason for this. If we were to have five categories with a 'central' one, for example a question such as 'Neither likely nor unlikely', then we have problems at the analysis stage. Unless the numbers in our questionnaire are very large, we will probably be forced into a position where we have to collapse our categories in order to get meaningful numbers to analyse. The obvious way to collapse the data is into those who think that smoking is quite likely or very likely to damage your health or those who think that smoking is not very likely or very unlikely to damage your health. If we were to have a neutral category then the replies to this have to be 'collapsed' into either the positive or the negative categories which weakens the force of the question. On the other hand, it does present possibilities for manipulating the results to say what we want to say – 'only 20% are opposed' may be disguising 30% who are in support of a proposition and 50% who answer 'Do not know'!
- If the numbers replying to the questionnaire are likely to be large, say in the order of 200 or more, then having three or five categories might be quite acceptable. But the smaller the total number of replies, the more important it is that we choose categories that can

be collapsed into broader expressions of opinion that contain enough cases for legitimate statistical analysis.

● Notice also the use of 'white space' in that the questions are not bunched together. Putting each question in its own box also helps to focus the respondents to one question at a time. Questionnaire layout is a question of aesthetics and judgement – what is required is a document which is easy to fill in and also facilitates the efficient transfer of data into the computer system.

THE WORDING OF QUESTIONS

Whole books have been written on the subject of the wording of questions in questionnaires. The aim should be, of course, to produce questions that are clear, that do not invite a particular pattern of response ('leading questions') and that mean broadly the same to all of the respondents. Many people believe that asking questions in a questionnaire is simple – it is not. Great care and thought should be taken over the selection of questions and this will generally be repaid by a better quality of answer.

A few simple rules are given below.

(a) *Keep questions simple, clear and concise.* It is possible to make questions too long and tortuous. Try to limit the number of words in the question and keep the language as simple and as clear as possible.

(b) *Ask only one question at a time.* It is possible that you are asking two questions at once without realizing it. For example, in a questionnaire on food-buying habits a question such as 'How often do you buy tea and coffee?' is asking two questions disguised as one.

(c) *Avoid 'leading' questions that invite a particular response.* It is very difficult to write questions that are completely neutral. Even a simple question such as 'What do you most enjoy about your job?' (followed by a list) has the implicit assumption built into it that there **are** some features that people enjoy about their jobs. Making a 'neutral' statement and then inviting people to agree or disagree, strongly or moderately (as in the questionnaire fragment above), is one way of avoiding a leading question.

A classic example of how a subtle bias may creep in is the question asked in Britain's only referendum in recent times. Two alternatives are presented with only one word of difference between the two. The second alternative is the question that was actually asked:

● 'Should Britain be a member of the European Economic Community?'

● 'Should Britain remain a member of the European Economic Community?'

(Notice that the only difference is the verb 'remain' rather than 'be', which, it could be argued, appealed to the innate conservatism of the electorate to leave things as they are.)

(d) *Avoid negative questions.* A double negative can cause confusion. Imagine the following question:

'Soft drugs should not be decriminalized'
Do you   *Agree* [   ]   *Disagree* [   ]

The respondent has to think carefully about the question before answering. Turning the question into a positive question ('The use of soft drugs should remain unlawful') is one way round this dilemma.

(e) *Keep the language as unambiguous as possible.* Even in the same society, different words may have somewhat different meanings such as 'dinner', 'tea', 'professional' and so on. Being aware of this is one way of avoiding the problem.

(f) *Is the question too precise?* Do not ask for a degree of precision which is not required. We are often interested not in a person's precise age as such but rather into what age group they fall. Similarly, we might not need a precise salary but the salary band into which they would place themselves and so on. Producing a band or a category into which individuals can place themselves is a way of avoiding embarrassment or refusal to answer a question. Questions on income are best dealt with in this way, as they are often a sensitive issue.

SOME PROBLEMS WITH QUESTIONNAIRE DESIGN

The 'Do not know' problem

There is a perennial problem with how to deal with the *'Do not know'* type of response. In fact, ticking a *'Do not know'* box can mean one of the following:

- 'I genuinely do not know the answer to the question'
- 'I do know the answer but I do not want to tell you'
- 'I do not understand the question!'
- The information will take too much time or trouble to find out so the safest response may be *'Do not know'*

and so on. The questionnaire designer has to weigh up whether it is worth including *'Do not know'* categories in the questions or whether to attempt to 'nudge' respondents into one of the categories that are provided. Again, there is no easy answer to this problem.

Question sequencing

Another problem is the sequencing of questions. The advice that is generally offered is that 'biographical' questions can often be left until the end of the questionnaire. The questionnaire should start with the most straightforward questions and build gradually towards those that might require more thought to answer correctly. More difficult or sensitive questions need placing appropriately. Generally, these should be well into the body of the interview but not left until the very end where they may leave an overall feeling of dissatisfaction with the questionnaire as a whole.

Response set

Psychologists are aware of what is termed the 'response set'. If you are setting a series of questions in which you are inviting agreement/ disagreement, then it is possible to get a series of answers in which the respondent has evidently ticked all of the 'Agree' or all of the 'Disagree' boxes. In order to avoid this problem, it is suggested that the wording of questions should be varied so that a 'positive' response is not always to agree with the question.

Multiple responses

A 'multiple' response is one in which respondents are invited to tick as many items in a list as they like. For example, one might be presented with a list of common foodstuffs and asked how many of them are bought each week:

How many of the following do you buy at least once a week?

(1)	Fresh fruit	[ ]
(2)	Fresh vegetables	[ ]
(3)	Tea	[ ]
(4)	Sugar	[ ]
(5)	Meat	[ ]
(6)	Fish	[ ]
(7)	Eggs	[ ]

In general terms, this type of question is a nightmare to analyse statistically and is best avoided, if at all possible. How, for example, does one represent an answer in which items 1, 3, 6 and 7 have all been ticked?

If this type of question cannot be avoided, then at the analysis stage the question is best considered as a series of seven short questions, each of which has a 'yes' or 'no' response. An example of how this might be done is shown below:

In the last week, did you buy FRESH FRUIT?   Yes [   ]   No [   ]

In the last week, did you buy FRESH VEGETABLES? Yes [   ]   No [   ]

---

and so on. This might seem rather long winded and repetitive but it is the only feasible way in which you can enter the data into a computer system for subsequent analysis.

The pre-test stage

Designing a questionnaire is more of an art than a science. It is best to try a policy of 'progressive refinement' – having composed the questionnaire, 'sleep on it' and the following day see if any of the questions could be altered somewhat to be clearer, more direct or less ambiguous. The most important principle of all is to 'pre-test' the questionnaire **before** the final version is agreed and printed. Even if it is tried out only on friends and relatives, the researcher can be alerted to questions that potentially are going to cause problems at the analysis stage or that seem to be capable of misinterpretation. Remember that the pre-test stage is generally your last opportunity to perfect your questionnaire before you run up the considerable expense of printing off the multiple copies that will be needed.

The TURBOSTATS package

4

WHAT IS TURBOSTATS?

TURBOSTATS is the name given to a suite of computer programs designed to work with each other in order to analyse social survey data, especially from questionnaires. Each of the programs may run as a 'stand-alone' program or as part of an integrated system. The TURBOSTATS system is closely modelled upon SPSS (Statistical Package for the Social Sciences) and is designed to give output similar to that offered by the SPSS 'Frequencies' and 'Cross-tabulation' commands.

The analysis of survey material, as we have already seen, tends to fall into the following categories.

Frequency distributions

These are the counts and percentages of the various values taken by a single variable – for example, those ticking a 'Yes' box or a 'No' box in reply to a question.

Contingency (cross-tabulation) tables

Tables are typically formed by evaluating two variables at the same time – for example, we might wish to see how responses to a particular question vary by sex. The contingency table computes the number of values which fall into each 'cell' as well as giving us the other statistics that we wish to specify – normally percentages.

Descriptive statistics

Variables which are said to be continuous (age, salary, heights, weights) can be analysed using conventional statistical measures.

A family of statistics known as 'parametric statistics' can be applied to these variables because if they follow what statisticians call a normal distribution (a bell-shaped curve) then we can estimate various values in the general population from the results of our sample.

Notice that these kinds of variables can also be put into categories. For many purposes, it is more convenient to put age and salary into some broad bands and then to work with these bands as though they were categorical rather than continuous variables, even though some of the detail may be lost by doing so.

Measures of association

Sometimes we wish to see whether two variables appear to vary with each other, either directly or inversely. We are then interested in a 'correlation coefficient'. If we are interested in trying to predict one variable once we are given the other variable (e.g. can we predict on the basis of past expenditure patterns what a family will spend upon food given its level of income) then we may well be interested in a regression equation.

Hypothesis test

The more sophisticated types of statistical analysis involve hypothesis testing. Using these techniques, we can tell whether a difference that we observe in the means of two continuous variables, such as salaries, could have occurred by chance or is said to be **statistically significant**. Applying the same logic to a contingency table (e.g. a 2 × 2 table with 'Sex' on one axis and 'Voting' on the other) would help us to discern whether there were statistically significant differences by sex in the ways in which the electorate voted.

HOW DOES TURBOSTATS WORK?

In order to function, each of the TURBOSTATS modules requires two files of data, as follows.

Datafiles

A datafile consists purely of numbers, separated from each other by spaces, commas or semicolons. Such a file is often known as a CSV (Comma Separated Value) file. An example is:

```
1,2,3
1,4,5
2,6,2
⋮
etc.
```

Labels files

A labels file is a text file which 'explains' to the TURBOSTATS system how to label the various numbers that it finds in the datafile. If we have a variable called SEX then the typical values might be that 1 stands for 'Female' whilst 2 stands for 'Male'.

These files can be created in several ways. For fairly small surveys, for example 100 cases or less, you could use the TS-ENTRY module. For larger surveys, it is often more cost effective in terms of time to input the data using a database program such as dBASE III/IV and to get the database to create the datafile for you with the appropriate command. In the case of dBASE this would be:

COPY TO filename.ext DELIMITED

It is also possible to create the datafile and the labels file by using your favourite word-processor or text editor, using it to write the relevant files in 'plain ASCII' mode. In WordStar, you would use 'Non-Document' mode, for example. (A simple but effective Word-Star compatible text editor, **TE.EXE**, is provided with the TURBO-STATS system.) If you use a text editor or word-processor, data input will be faster but you will not have the benefit of any error-checking or correction facilities. A labels file might look like the following:

```
"SEX", "Gender of individual"
"SEX", "Female"
"SEX", "Male"
"CLASS", "Social class"
"CLASS", "Professional"
"CLASS", "Skilled manual"
"CLASS", "Semi-skilled manual"
"CLASS", "Unskilled manual"
⋮
etc.
```

The TURBOSTATS system will assume that the first variable name encountered in a labels file relates to the first column of data found in a datafile. Similarly, the second variable found will relate to the second column of data and so on. Care should be taken to ensure that the variable names match up with the various columns of numbers as TURBOSTATS has no way of 'knowing', other than by position in a list, which variable names match up with which columns of data.

The labels work in a similar fashion. Once the TURBOSTATS system has identified the 'starting point' in the labels file, then the following are assumed.

- The first entry will be a label which expands upon the name of the variable – this is known as a VARIABLE LABEL. For example, the variable name MINCOME might be a variable which you wish to label as "Mother's income".
- Each subsequent label relates to the various values taken by the variable and consequently these are known as VALUE labels. The labels should cover the complete range of the values from minimum to maximum that are likely to be encountered in the data set.

In this respect, TURBOSTATS does not differ significantly from the SPSS philosophy where two files of data are also required.

THE TURBOSTATS MODULES

The TURBOSTATS system provides three modules designed for the analysis of survey data (TS-FREQ1, TS-CROSS and TS-STATS) and a further two to assist in the entry and editing of datafiles (TS-ENTRY, TS-CASES). In addition, some utility programs are provided, the most important of which captures screen outputs which are then converted into text files for subsequent incorporation into your written report. Provision is also made for you to access your favourite spreadsheet package if you wish to process data in a graphical form.

Each of the TURBOSTATS modules will now be briefly described.

TS-FREQ1

This module provides a frequency distribution of the values of a single variable measured at the categorical (nominal) level. This module is best used to analyse the patterns of response to a single question. The output consists of counts, percentages, valid percentages (once 'missing values' have been ignored), cumulative percentages and a simple bar chart. It is possible to save these results in a file should you wish to import these later into a graphics package for further analysis.

TS-CROSS

When we wish to form simple tables of the joint distribution of two nominal variables (e.g. sex and voting behaviour) then we utilize this module. At its simplest, TS-CROSS provides simple counts of the number of cases that fall into each 'cell' in the table. However, it can also generate column percentages, row percentages, total percentages, the statistically 'expected' value and the chi-square values for each cell in the table if we so request.

TS-STATS

This is the module which provides the more specialized statistical information required for either one or two variables. It assumes that data is measured at the continuous level (but will not report an error if asked to analyse data measured at the nominal level – for example, being asked to produce an average of a series of ones and twos which are coding numbers for perhaps 'Yes' and 'No' responses). If two variables are specified, then TS-STATS assumes that you wish to calculate a range of bivariate statistics including the correlation coefficient, the regression equation and a 't'-test for the differences in the means. It is also possible to use this module to perform tests of statistical significance ('t'-tests) on sub-groupings within a variable. For example, it would be possible to discover whether the mean income for 'Females' might differ statistically from the mean income for 'Males' in a data set. It is also possible to display histograms of the variables and a scatter plot of the joint distribution of the two variables.

TS-ENTRY

Unlike the previous three modules, TS-ENTRY does not calculate any output for you. Rather, you can use it to create the files for:

* the variable and label names (the labels file);
* the input of the numerical data (the datafile).

When you use this module, you need to create your labels file first. This is then used so that the variable names can supply the prompts for the various values as you input the numerical data.

To simplify the operation of TS-ENTRY, the module is not designed to alter or to modify existing labels files. If modifications are minor, this is best achieved using your favourite word-processor or text editor in 'plain ASCII' mode. In the event of major modifications, you would be well advised to create a brand-new labels file in any case.

TS-CASES

Finally, this module splits your data to create sub-files for more detailed analysis. For example, you may wish to create a file containing only 'Females' so that you can examine further relationships within the data.

INSTALLING AND RUNNING TURBOSTATS

Installing TURBOSTATS

IMPORTANT! Before you start any installation procedure, make a backup copy of your disk using the DISKCOPY command from DOS. Put your original away in a safe place and then work ONLY from your copy.

If you intend to run TURBOSTATS from your hard disk, then:

- create a sub-directory of your choice on the hard disk with the command
  MD (Make Directory), e.g. MD\TS
- change to that sub-directory with the command CD\TS
- copy all of the files over from the distribution disk
  copy a:*.*   [or b:*.*]
- activate the program by typing TS. The program automatically installs itself the first time it is run.

If you intend to run TURBOSTATS directly from the distribution floppy then merely type TS.

Running TURBOSTATS

When you run TURBOSTATS you will first be given some preliminary information concerning how you are to save the screens that you generate as 'snapshots'. These snapshots give you the facility to incorporate output into your written documents, and as they are text files they can be edited in the same way as any other text file.

After the opening screen, you are presented with the opening menu:

TS-MENU		TURBOSTATS	(c) M. C. Hart [1992]
Module	[1] **TS-FREQ1**	Frequencies of one variable [NOMINAL level]	
Module	[2] **TS-CROSS**	Cross-tabulations of two variables [NOMINAL level]	
Module	[3] **TS-STATS**	Statistics and plots of one or two variables [NOMINAL or INTERVAL level]	
Module	[4] **TS-ENTRY**	Data and label entry	
Module	[5] **TS-CASES**	Create sub-files for particular cases	
Module	[6] **SD**	Sorted Directory	
Module	[7] **Load**	Program of your own choice, e.g. a spreadsheet	

Choose Options Numbers [1] to [7] [X] to exit   **CTRL-BRK to abort**

From this opening menu, you choose an option number (without even pressing ENTER) and the module will then load and run. If you have chosen the wrong one or wish to abort a particular analysis then **CTRL-BREAK** will exit you from the module and take you back to the opening menu. Some other options, not shown on the menu, are also available for the more advanced user. See p. 101 for further details.

PREPARING AND ENTERING YOUR DATA

At this stage, we shall explore ways of getting some data into the system for TURBOSTATS to analyse. Remember that TURBOSTATS, in common with other statistical packages, can only cope with datafiles that consist of **numbers** and your questionnaire or survey instrument should be designed so that this is the end product.

The datafile

Whichever TURBOSTATS analysis module you choose, the system will need a datafile of numbers presented to it. Let us imagine a very small questionnaire completed by ten students. The type of questions asked are as follows:

STUDENT PROFILE Questionnaire	
Please put a tick [✔] in one box **only**	*Office use only*
Q1. Are you: (1) Female [ ] (2) Male [ ]	SEX [ ]
Q2. Would you define yourself as a SMOKER? (1) Yes [ ] (2) No [ ]	SMOKER [ ]
Q3. Do you hold a full driving licence? (1) Yes [ ] (2) No [ ]	LICENCE [ ]
Q4. How much GRANT do you receive or expect to receive each term? [ ][ ][ ][ ]	GRANT

The datafile that we wish to produce will look like this:

```
1,2,1,295
2,2,1,585
1,2,2,130
2,2,2,470
2,2,2,690
1,2,2,525
2,2,1, 80
1,1,2,375
2,1,1,690
2,1,1,600
```

Each **row** in this table will correspond to one completed questionnaire whilst each **column** will represent the answers to a single question. As row 1 contains the figures 1,2,1,295 then this represents an answer from a student who is Female (coded 1), a Non-smoker (coded 2), has a driving licence (coded 1) and who has a termly grant of £295.

If you have a small questionnaire, then it is a good idea to transfer all of the data from the questionnaires to one or two sheets of paper – let us call this a **data matrix**. This can be done at home, or at least before you start to approach the computer system.

To produce our datafile, we can use several methods.

- Use a **database** such as dBASE III/IV. In dBASE, one would create a database, enter the data and finally copy it to a datafile with the command:

    COPY TO filename.ext DELIMITED

- Use a text editor. A simple public domain text editor is provided with the TURBOSTATS system (**TE.EXE**).
- Use the TS-ENTRY module (but this requires a labels file to be composed first).
- Use a spreadsheet and then export the data in an ASCII file mode. In SuperCalc, for example, one would print the data to a file rather than to a printer. The same technique can be used with the **TC.EXE** simple spreadsheet supplied with the TURBOSTATS system.

If you do decide to use a text editor to prepare your data, then make the data **rectangular**. By this we mean making the data line up neatly in columns as this makes it so much easier to check in the case of errors. An example is shown in the seventh line of the datafile shown above.

Having produced your datafile, it is a good idea to obtain a printout of it so that you can check that each column seems to contain the correct kind of data. For example, if we had values other than a 1 or 2 in the SEX column, then there could well be an error in the data, as could a value of only 1 or 2 in the GRANT column.

The labels file

In order to interpret the numerical data, TURBOSTATS requires a labels file. This will make the output much more meaningful – what became coded as a 1 or 2 in the SEX question in our questionnaire can now be re-interpreted as meaning 'Female' and 'Male' in our output.

The labels file that corresponds with the datafile above will look like this:

"SEX", "Student gender"
"SEX", "Female"
"SEX", "Male"
"SMOKER", "Smoking behaviour"
"SMOKER", "Smoker"
"SMOKER", "Non-smoker"
"DRIVER", "Holds a full driving licence"
"DRIVER", "Yes"
"DRIVER", "No"
"GRANT", "Grant per term"

There are several features to note about the labels file.

- Each variable is designated by a variable name which is a maximum of eight letters long and must be in CAPITAL letters. This variable name is used by the TURBOSTATS system in the analysis modules and is the way in which one **column** of data can be selected for analysis.
- The first line of a series of variable names explains to the user what the variable name stands for. A name of eight letters can be rather cryptic and certainly not self-explanatory, and for this reason the system allows you to give a label of up to 25 characters to help to 'explain' the meaning of the variable. In the labels file above, for example, the variable 'DRIVER' is given a variable label which explains that it actually means 'Holds a full driving licence'. The variable labels are often in effect truncated

versions of the actual questions of which the original can be found in the questionnaire.

- After the first line in each group, which we have seen is devoted to the variable labels, come the value labels. The value labels are not numbered but the assumption in the TURBOSTATS system is that the first in the list will correspond to a value of 1, the second to a value of 2 and so on up to a maximum of 9. You are allowed to have up to nine categories only, which should be sufficient for most purposes. Otherwise, group some categories together to keep within the overall limit.
- The **value labels** can only be up to 15 characters long. This may seem to be a little restrictive but there is a good reason for it. When we come to perform a frequency distribution or, even more so, to form contingency tables, there is only a limited amount of space available. In the case of contingency tables, the value labels are 'wrapped around' since the available space in each cell is only six characters wide. So keep variable names as short and succinct as possible. Although spaces are not technically illegal in the variable labels, it is much better practice to avoid them if possible. We can use the underline character (_) to simulate a space and this makes the name so much more readable. For example, if we wished to compose a variable name for 'Father's income' then a good choice could well be 'F_INCOME'.
- Notice that the variable name and the variable label are separated from each by a comma with no spaces on either side of it. Any variable or value labels which are too long will be truncated (i.e. cut down) to the allowable lengths.
- It is important that the variable names are in block capital letters and that the (repeated) variable names are spelled exactly the same. The TURBOSTATS system looks down the list of names to determine where one column of data ends and another one starts. As soon as one name differs from another (even if the result of a typing error) then the system will assume that it has encountered another variable.

Trouble shooting

The TURBOSTATS system must be presented with datafiles and labels files that 'match up' with each other in order to get the anticipated results. A reminder is now given of how the two files should relate to each other:

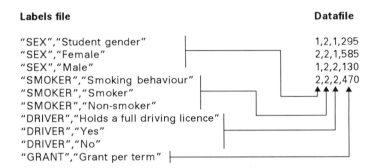

Labels file	Datafile
"SEX","Student gender"	1,2,1,295
"SEX","Female"	2,2,1,585
"SEX","Male"	1,2,2,130
"SMOKER","Smoking behaviour"	2,2,2,470
"SMOKER","Smoker"	
"SMOKER","Non-smoker"	
"DRIVER","Holds a full driving licence"	
"DRIVER","Yes"	
"DRIVER","No"	
"GRANT","Grant per term"	

When you are entering data, particularly with a text editor, it is important that each line of data ends with a carriage return/line feed (CR/LF). These bytes should be present at the end of every line – they are termed 'non-printing characters' and may not be visible. If the word-processor or text editor that you use can display the CR/LF bytes diagrammatically (e.g. dBASE and WordStar use the '<' symbol), then this helps to ensure that your data is in the form that TURBOSTATS expects to find it. It is also important that you do not have blank lines either at the beginning or at the end of your output. If the system appears to 'hang' (i.e. the keyboard becomes entirely unresponsive to the user) once you have specified the datafiles and labels files, then it is almost certain that you have something in these files which is causing the problem. Following the instructions carefully should eliminate the problem.

Missing cases

In all surveys, there is always the problem of deciding what to do with those sections of the questionnaire that have been missed out or not filled in correctly. To cope with this quite common situation, the analyst generally allocates a code number (known as a 'Missing Value' code) so that the system 'knows' to exclude these from the rest of the data. You may use practically any integer as a code value assuming that it does not occur in the data. A common choice is to use a negative number such as –1, –9 or –999. A good choice would be to decide that you are never going to use the value of zero and to have this as the code for your missing value. When the system asks in various places for a missing value, then a missing value of zero will be supplied by default if you just press ENTER, so for reasons of speed a zero is a good choice.

Frequency distributions   5

We have already met examples of the ways in which we can examine the responses to a single question. The TURBOSTATS module that we use is TS-FREQ1, so-called to remind us that we use this module to examine only one variable at a time.

USING THE TS-FREQ1 MODULE

Many simple questions could be analysed by using the TS-FREQ1 module alone. When analysing a questionnaire, probably the first step is to perform a frequency distribution of each of the questions that lends itself to such an analysis. These will be all of those questions in which the answers are given simple coding numbers, typically in the range of 1–9.

Having chosen Module 1 from the Opening Menu, we are then presented with the following screen:

TS-FREQ1   **TURBOSTATS**   (c) M. C. Hart [1992]
~~~~~~~~~~   ~~~~~~~~~~~~~~   ~~~~~~~~~~~~~~~~~~~

Performs frequency counts, barcharts of raw (nominal) data..
Name of raw data file   ? b:mysurvey.txt
Name of labels file   ? b:labels.txt

The user input is underlined. Here we have a datafile which is called MYSURVEY.TXT (on Drive B:) and a labels file which is called LABELS.TXT (also on Drive B:).

The TURBOSTATS system will assume that all of your datafiles and labels files have the extension of '.txt'. So, if you like, you can ignore the .txt extension if your files have this extension in the first place.

The datafiles will be located and read. If all goes well, then the next screen presented to the user is:

TS-FREQ1   **TURBOSTATS**   **File: B:MYSURVEY.TXT**
~~~~~~~~   ~~~~~~~~~~~~   ~~~~~~~~~~~~~~~~~~~~~~

Performs frequency counts, barcharts of raw (nominal) data..

Variable List - [Y]es or [N]o .. [X] to exit Y

ID   SEX   CLASS   PAPER   SALARY   P_INCOME

Variable ? sex

Missing Values should be integers in the range-128 .. 127 e.g. [0] [9] [-1]
                                                          [0 by default]
Missing Values for SEX   0

The user input is again underlined. The first choice is whether to see the variable list or not. The answer to this is almost invariably [Y]es, so the user merely presses Y – there is no need to press ENTER. Then the user is prompted to type in the variable name. This needs to be typed in full and followed by ENTER. Finally, the user should specify the Missing Values for this variable (or just press ENTER to select a zero by default).

The user should now get the first page of output:

| SEX   Sex of Individual | | | | File: B:MYSURVEY.TXT | |
Value Label	Value	Frequency	Percent	Valid Percent	Cum Percent
Male	1	102	51.0	52.0	52.0
Female	2	94	47.0	48.0	100.0
	0	4	2.0	MISSING	
	TOTAL	200	100.0	100.0	

Male ■■■■■■■■■■■■■■■■■■■■ 102
Female ■■■■■■■■■■■■■■■■■■ 94

Valid Cases   196   Missing Cases   4

EXPLANATION OF THE OUTPUT

- Near the top of the screen, notice that we have the variable name and also the variable label. These have evidently been taken from the labels file. On the right-hand side, we also have the name of the datafile that is being used.
- Now follows various columns of output. In the first column we have the value labels (again taken from the labels file). The adjacent column is headed 'Value' and what is presented here are the presumed coding numbers for the data, starting at 1 and counting up as far as the total number of categories that have been found. Then we have the 'Frequency' column which is probably the most significant of all. This contains the 'raw counts' of the data – here we have 102 Males and 94 Females. Notice also that we have 4 people who did not reply, or replied incorrectly. These values have a code value of 0.
- Having counted up the 'raw data', the next two columns compute percentages for us. The first column labelled 'Percent' gives us the crude percentage for every value, including the missing values – we can see that as there are 4 missing cases, and as there are 200 cases this is evidently 2%. However, the missing values 'get in the way' of the analysis. We are really only interested in those cases in which the respondents have answered correctly. So the next column is labelled 'Valid Percent' and this column works out the percentages based upon the 196 who did reply. The final percentage column is labelled 'Cum Percent'. This is the **cumulative**

percentage column and it works by keeping a running total of the responses until it arrives at 100%. This is not very meaningful when we only have two categories in the data as we have here. If, however, we were to have four categories as follows:

1 'Very much dislike'   3 'Like'
2 'Dislike'   4 'Very much like'

then the cumulative percentage will come into its own. We will be able to see the total percentages that come into categories 1 and 2 (i.e. the **disliking** responses) or by subtraction from 100% those categories that come into the **liking** responses.

- If there is room on the screen, the user will also see a simple diagrammatic representation of the data in the form of a sideways bar chart. This is intended only to give a rough 'feel' for the data on the principle that 'a picture is worth a thousand words'. If there is no room on this screen for the bar chart, then the user should press ENTER and the bar chart will then be displayed on the following screen. No instructions are given to this effect so that the screen output is kept uncluttered for those occasions when you want to capture this screen for your printed output.
- Finally, we are given an indication of the total number of valid cases in the datafile, as well as those coded with missing values. The total number of cases (200 in this example) is given under the 'TOTAL' row of the 'Frequency' column.

CAPTURING THE OUTPUT

We can view the results of our frequency distribution on the screen but there are two ways in which we can 'capture' the output for later use. These are detailed below.

Capturing the output with a 'screen print'

MS-DOS users will be aware that if they press the key labelled **PrtSc** and they have a printer connected and on-line, then the contents of their screens will be dumped on to the printer. The TURBOSTATS package reprograms the use of the **PrtSc** key and diverts it for its own purposes. Now when you press this key, a copy of the screen will be 'snapped' (as though you were taking a photograph) and the contents are held in memory. The computer will give a beep and the caption SNAPSHOT.01 will appear near the top right-hand corner of the screen. You may take up to 30 snapshots in a single session.

When you finish the TURBOSTATS session, another piece of software will take the 'snapshots' that have been taken and will convert them into files, named SNAPSHOT.01 up to SNAPSHOT.30. As these are text files you can incorporate them into whatever report you have to write and you may edit them at will.

Saving the values in a file

If you would like to feed your results into a spreadsheet, then this is also possible. If you press ENTER after having viewed your results then the following dialogue will occur. The user input is underlined.

> Save results in output file [Y]es [N]o? y
>
> Drive (e.g. A: B: C:)? B:
>
> Save results in B:CLASS.TXT [Y]es [N]o? y
>
> Results now saved in B:CLASS.TXT

As you can see, the results will be saved in a file which has the same filename as the variable and the extension of .TXT. You have the choice of using another filename if you wish.

The results of the variable CLASS will appear like this when you use the DOS command TYPE CLASS.TXT:

"Label"	"Value"	"Frequency"	"Percent"	"Valid%"	"Cumul%"
"Professional"	1	42	14.0	14.6	14.6
"Intermediate"	2	22	7.3	7.7	22.3
"Skilled manual"	3	37	12.3	12.9	35.2
"Semi-skilled manual"	4	53	17.7	18.5	53.7
"Unskilled manual"	5	66	22.0	23.0	76.7
"Pensioners"	6	29	9.7	10.1	86.8
"Not classified"	7	38	12.7	13.2	100.0

In this form, they may be read into a spreadsheet. For example, if you use the popular Lotus 1-2-3 clone 'ASEASYAS' then you would follow this procedure. The spreadsheet menus will respond to you typing in the letter designated in the square brackets:

/ [F]ile   [D]irectory B:\{ENTER}
/ [I]mport [V]alues CLASS.TXT

Once you have read the data into the spreadsheet, then you can use the facilities offered there to draw a superior bar chart or pie chart.

USING TS-FREQ1 TO CHECK ON YOUR DATAFILES AND LABELS FILES

The only way to be sure that your datafiles and labels files are going to give the results that you intend is to use them in one of the TURBOSTATS modules. TS-FREQ1 is a good way in which you can check that the datafiles and the labels files correctly 'match up' with each other. Whilst you can only check on the categorical and not the continuous variables in this module, it will none the less provide a speedy way of ensuring that all is well. If you do choose a continuous variable by mistake, TURBOSTATS will inform you that the numbers are out of range and invite you to choose again.

Contingency tables

6

In the preceding chapter, we examined how we can look at one variable at a time in a frequency distribution. Very often in a survey, we want to examine two variables at a time and to do this we form a **contingency table**. Contingency tables can only be formed from variables measured at the nominal or categorical level, exactly like frequency distributions. The most common form is a '2 by 2' table in which two variables, each of which can take one of two values, form the axes of the table. For example, we might have a table in which we have SEX ('Female', 'Male') and DRIVER ('Holds licence', 'Does not hold licence') in which case we would form a table with four cells in it.

USING THE TS-CROSS MODULE

The procedure is very similar in operation to the TS-FREQ1 module except this time we shall be prompted to choose **two** variables. Having selected item 2 from the Opening Menu, the initial input screen will look like this:

TS-CROSS   **TURBOSTATS**   **File: B:MYSURVEY.TXT**

Constructs contingency tables from raw (nominal) data..

Variable List - [Y]es or [N]o .. [X] to exit <u>Y</u>

ID   SEX   CLASS   PAPER   SALARY

First variable ?   <u>sex</u>
Second variable ?   <u>class</u>

Missing Values should be integers in the range -128 .. 127
    e.g. [0] [9] [-1] [0 by default]

Missing Values for SEX   <u>0</u>

Missing Values for CLASS <u>0</u>

The user input is again underlined.

Notice how, having specified the two variables in which we are interested, we need to specify the 'Missing Values' in each case.

Once the files have been located and their contents read into the system, the next screen to appear is the following:

The data is now entered..

In the contingency table, you have a choice of options as well as the cell counts

These are   [1]   Row percentages
             [2]   Column percentages
             [3]   Total percentages
             [4]   Expected values
             [5]   Chi-square statistic

If you want to choose the option, then give the OPTION number when prompted. Options will be printed in the order you specify..
Specify 0 if you do NOT want the option..

        First Choice   [Option No]   0
        Second Choice   [Option No]   0
        Third Choice   [Option No]   0
        Fourth Choice   [Option No]   0
        Fifth Choice   [Option No]   0

This screen gives the user the option of what to put in each cell as well as the pure counts.

- **Row percentages** give the percentage of the count in the cell expressed as a proportion of the total in the **row**.
- **Column percentages** give the percentage of the count in the cell expressed as a proportion of the total in the **column**. Information presented as column percentages is often easier to absorb than the same information presented as a row percentage.
- **Total percentages** give the percentage of the count in the cell expressed as a proportion of the total numbers in the entire table. This is often less useful than either the row or total percentages.
- **Expected values**. The expected value is computed by TURBOSTATS and is used typically with the chi-square statistic which follows it. Even without the chi-square, it can be used as a quick check to see if there appear to be any differences in the data. The way in which the expected value is worked out is best illustrated by an example. If we have 70 drivers in our sample of 100 and there are 50 females and 50 males in the sample, then the number of female (and male) drivers that we would expect is $70 \times (50/100)$ or 35.
- **Chi-square statistic.** This is a specialized statistic used predominantly in contingency tables to see if there is a statistical difference in the distribution of the two variables. It is usually represented by

the Greek letter χ^2, pronounced 'kie' as in 'pie'. For example, whilst there might be slight differences in the proportions of female and male drivers that we observe in our sample, at what point do we know that the differences are sufficiently large to achieve what statisticians call **statistical significance**? The answer lies in getting a p-value (probability value) of less than 0.05 (5 chances in a 100 that the differences could have occurred by chance).

To choose any or all of these options we merely press the relevant number. The options will appear in the cell in the order in which we press the option and therefore we have some control over how the output will appear. There is no need to press ENTER as you choose the option numbers. When you have selected your last option, the contingency table will be calculated and will then appear.

EXPLANATION OF THE OUTPUT

We shall illustrate first the most basic case where we are concerned only with the basic counts that fall into each cell:

Crosstabulation of SEX	By CLASS	Sex of Individual	Social Class		File: B:MYSURVEY.TXT			
CLASS >	Profes sional	Interm ediate	Skille d Manu	Semi-s killed	Unskil led Ma	Pensio ners	Not cl assifi	ROW TOTAL
SEX	1	2	3	4	5	6	7	
Male 1	16	12	10	16	22	2	20	98
Female 2	12	4	14	16	24	14	8	92
TOTAL	28	16	24	32	46	16	28	190
	14.7%	8.4%	12.6%	16.8%	24.2%	8.4%	14.7%	100.0%

Valid cases = 190   Missing = 10

A contingency table is also known as a **cross-tabulation** table. By examining the table above, you will notice various features:

- Notice how the value labels are 'wrapped around' each column heading. In order to accommodate a reasonable number of cells on a single screen, the cells are only six spaces wide and therefore the value labels are truncated to 12 characters and are 'wrapped around' as a heading for each column. Therefore the shorter the value labels the better, which is a point worth bearing in mind when the labels file is created.

• Notice also how, even in a simple cross-tabulation table like this one, the numbers in each column and row are totalled up – these are known as the **marginal** totals. Even though you have not requested it, the column totals are expressed as a percentage of the total as this is the statistic which is most used in a table of this type.

• Your table is limited to a total of nine cells in each direction, giving a maximum number of 81 cells. If you find that you do not have enough space to display all of the rows of data then pressing ENTER will display the rest of the table on the next screen. Remember to 'snap' your screen first as once the second screen is displayed you cannot go back to the first screen without regenerating the table.

Now we shall see what the most complex type of contingency table looks like when we have chosen every option:

Crosstabulation of SEX By CLASS		Sex of Individual Social Class				File: B:MYSURVEY.TXT		
CLASS > SEX	Profes sional 1	Interm ediate 2	Skille d Manu 3	Semi-s killed 4	Unskil led Ma 5	Pensio ners 6	Not cl assifi 7	ROW TOTAL
Male 1	16	12	10	16	22	2	20	98
[Row%]	16.3	12.2	10.2	16.3	22.4	2.0	20.4	51.6%
[Col%]	57.1	75.0	41.7	50.0	47.8	12.5	71.4	
[Tot%]	8.4	6.3	5.3	8.4	11.6	1.1	10.5	
[Exp]	14.4	8.3	12.4	16.5	23.7	8.3	14.4	
[Chis]	0.2	1.7	0.5	0.0	0.1	4.7	2.1	
Female 2	12	4	14	16	24	14	8	92
[Row%]	13.0	4.3	15.2	17.4	26.1	15.2	8.7	48.4%
[Col%]	42.9	25.0	58.3	50.0	52.2	87.5	28.6	
[Tot%]	6.3	2.1	7.4	8.4	12.6	7.4	4.2	
[Exp]	13.6	7.7	11.6	15.5	22.3	7.7	13.6	
[Chis]	0.2	1.8	0.5	0.0	0.1	5.0	2.3	
TOTAL	28	16	24	32	46	16	28	190
	14.7%	8.4%	12.6%	16.8%	24.2%	8.4%	14.7%	100.0%

Valid cases = 190   Missing = 10
Total chi-square	D.F.	Significance	Cells with E.F.< 5
19.298	6	0.0037	0 of 14 (0.0%)

- This table is evidently much more complex than the preceding table which contained cell counts only. In practice, you would rarely need to make a table as complex as this but it is full of information. To interpret a table such as this, we shall take the top left-hand cell as a starting point. We can see that there are 16 'Professional Males'. The row percentage is worked out by 16/98*100 – this equals 16.3%. (In computing, the symbol '/' means divided by, whilst the symbol '*' means multiplied. '*' is chosen in preference to '×' to avoid ambiguity.) Therefore we know that 16.3% of all Males are Professionals. Similarly, we work out a column percentage by calculating 'Professional Males' as a proportion of the column of 'Professionals' – this is 16/28*100 = 57.1%. If we wished to know the total of 'Professional Males' in the whole sample, then this is 16/190*100 = 8.4%.

- We have previously met the figure that might be the 'Expected' figure. Knowing that the proportion of 'Professionals' in the whole sample is 28/190 and the total number of Males is 98, then the number of 'Professional Males' that we could expect if the distribution of social classes across the sexes was equal would be 28/190*98 = 14.4%.

  The chi-square statistic is worked out in the following way:

$$\frac{(\text{Observed} - \text{Expected})^2}{\text{Expected}}$$

We can see that if the 'Observed' and the 'Expected' are very similar to each other, then 'Observed – Expected', even when squared, will remain small. Hence the smaller the chi-square in a cell, the less the divergence of what we actually 'observe' in the sample from that which we would be led to 'expect'. By the same reasoning, the greater the chi-square in an individual cell, the greater the discrepancy between observed and expected. If you scan the 'Chis' row of the table quickly, you will see that the biggest chi-square reported by TS-CROSS is for 'Female Pensioners' in our sample. We would have expected to have found 7.7 but actually have 14 and this contributes to the large chi-square value of 5.0.

- You will notice additional output at the bottom of the cross-tabulation table if you have specified that you want the chi-square statistic. This calls for a degree of statistical knowledge for its interpretation. It is reproduced as:

Total chi-square	D.F.	Significance	Cells with E.F. < 5
19.298	6	0.0037	0 of 14 (0.0%)

The total chi-square figure is the addition of the chi-squares in the individual cells, thus producing a chi-square for the whole table.

• D.F. stands for 'Degrees of Freedom'. One very simple and non-technical explanation of this statistical concept is that it gives us a quick way of adjusting to the fact that tables of different sizes will generate different total chi-squares. For example, it is not a surprise if a 5 × 5 table with 25 cells has a larger chi-square figure than a 2 × 2 table with 4 cells. The 'Degree of Freedom' figure is worked by the formula:

(Rows – 1) * (Columns – 1)

As this table has two rows (Male, Female) and seven columns (Professional etc.) then the Degrees of Freedom will be

(2 – 1) * (7 – 1) = 1 * 6 = 6

• The next and most important figure for present purposes is the 'Significance' figure. Normally, having calculated our chi-square and computed the degrees of freedom, we would have to consult the table of chi-squares in a statistics textbook to find what our chi-square figure of 19.298 and 6 degrees of freedom actually mean.

• The TS-CROSS module saves you the effort by reporting the 'Significance' figure. This will take a value between 0 and 1. Statisticians will say that a result is 'statistically significant' if a value is attained of 0.05 or less. This means that there is 0.05/1 or 5% likelihood that this result could have occurred by chance. If there is only a 5% likelihood of having occurred by chance, then it follows that there is a 95% likelihood that the result that we obtain could not have occurred by chance. In other words, any figure less than 0.05 indicates that the differences we have observed between Males and Females in their Social Class composition are 'non-chance' differences. In this particular case, the significance is 0.0037. If we multiply this mentally by 100 to turn it into a percentage, then we see that there is a 0.37% chance that we could have obtained these results accidentally, for example by selecting a 'rogue sample'. As there is a 99.63% chance that these are not accidental results, we conclude that there **is** a sex difference in our sample.

- Computers can work out the calculations such as chi-square and its probability without a great deal of difficulty. What is much more difficult for the typical user is to know what the figures reported by the module actually mean. Significance testing is not an easy topic to grasp immediately and one has to 'train oneself' to look at the figures and see what information is being conveyed by them. However, to simplify the interpretation of the chi-square figure down to its barest essentials, all we have to remember is:

  Significance **less** than 0.05   **SIGNIFICANT** difference
  Significance in range 0.06–1.0   **NO SIGNIFICANT** difference

- The final element that we have to interpret is the 'Cells with E.F. < 5' statement. This means 'Cells with an Expected Frequency of less than 5 cases'. The TS-CROSS module reports this figure to you because the chi-square statistic, like many other statistics, relies upon various assumptions before its results can be interpreted correctly. One important assumption is that the total number of cells with an expected frequency of less than 5 should not be more than 20% of the total number of cells. The exact reasons for this cannot be dealt with here, but if you do get a figure in this region, then you know that you are violating some of the underlying assumptions of the chi-square and if you are relying upon this to report your findings then the results may be invalid. In a case like this, you would need to go 'back to the drawing board' and collapse some of the categories together so that each cell would have a significantly large number to analyse. In the example used above, for instance, we might collapse the seven social class groupings into three ('White collar workers', 'Blue collar workers', 'Not employed').

MORE COMPLEX ANALYSIS

Taken together with the frequency distribution, the cross-tabulation is one of the widely used means of reporting survey results. It is possible to conduct and analyse quite a complex survey using frequencies and cross-tabulations alone. As we have seen from the analysis above, we can use the cross-tabulation table to report the numbers of cases that we find or we can go further and perform a statistical test of the differences that we find.

There are times when we feel that we need to go further and split the data into further categories. If, for example, we were to find that there was a difference in salary levels between males and females then this might be explained by the fact that males are somewhat more likely than females to be educated to degree level. To ascertain the precise influence of sex on the one hand against education on the other hand, we would need to keep one factor constant whilst allowing another factor to vary. In this example, we would need to examine both males and females as separate samples. If we were to find that both males and females were educated to the same level, then we would have to conclude that the differences in salary levels that we observe were not the result of being educated to degree level *per se*. It could be that we have to investigate further – for example, women, having gained their degrees, might find they are disadvantaged in the labour market compared with men. A lot of social scientific analysis is concerned with trying to 'tease out' the possible combinations of factors or causal sequences that might account for the differences revealed in our survey results. We shall discover how to create sub-samples in Chapter 8.

WHAT DOES OUR CONTINGENCY TABLE TELL US?

When the chi-square statistic was being discussed previously, the concept of statistical significance was discussed briefly. However, just because data shows some significant differences it should not be taken to imply that we have discovered anything of any real importance. All that is being stated is that the data shows differences which we could well have predicted without the benefit of a survey. The obverse of this is equally true. If we find no significant differences, then this **could** be a source of great interest to us.

Let us illustrate this point with a simple example. We have taken a sample of students and measured their heights and weights. At the same time, we have asked questions to ascertain whether or not they have 'secretarial' skills such as word-processing.

Before we start to analyse the data, we might imagine that we would find that, on average, men are both heavier and taller than women. Given the bias in the educational curriculum and the labour market, we might also expect to find that more women than men define themselves as having 'secretarial skills'. In this hypothetical survey, we now analyse the data and find that, in **statistical** terms, our cross-tabulation surveys indicate:

- men are heavier (and taller) than women;
- there is no sex difference in the distribution of secretarial skills.

In the first case, we have discovered something that is **statistically** significant but of no real **social** significance. We could hardly rush into print, say in the *British Medical Journal,* to report our findings that men are heavier on average than women. Just because we have a finding that is **statistically** significant does not mean that we have anything to report.

However, the obverse case is even more interesting. If we would expect to find some differences but in practice find none, then the **absence** of statistical significance might be extremely telling, in social terms. It would tell us, for example, that sex differences in skills important in the labour market were becoming more evenly distributed between the sexes. There may well be the temptation to assume that just because we have found something that is **statistically** significant, then we have found something to report of more social significance, and if we do not find anything of statistical significance, there is nothing to report at all. A moment's reflection will reveal that **statistical** significance and **social** significance are not the same thing at all. Indeed, the most important point to emerge from a survey may be the **absence** rather than the **presence** of significant differences.

The researcher needs to be aware of this important distinction before the analysis of the survey is written up. The statistical tools are only an aid to the analysis and not a substitute for it. It also takes a certain amount of experience to judge that the absence of a statistically significant difference may be an extremely important research finding. If the researcher is interested in testing out such relationships, then stating the research hypothesis (even if only in the form of stating what they would expect to find) is a good way of being alerted to the important distinctions between **statistical** and **social** significance.

Analysis of continuous variables $\quad$ 7

So far, we have been examining the responses to questionnaires that have been coded into simple categories such as 1, 2 or 3. Remember that these 'numbers' are not really numbers at all but merely convenient 'labels' that we append to different categories of data. This, in turn, facilitates the task for whatever software we are utilizing to analyse the data. There are occasions, however, when we collect data in the form of 'real' numbers such as a height, weight or a salary. These are numbers that form a 'continuous stream' – when plotted on a graph, they often form a 'bell-shaped' curve and are known as a 'normal distribution'. To analyse data in this form we shall now use the TS-STATS module.

USING THE TS-STATS MODULE

When using this module, we have the choice of specifying either one or two variables. If we specify one variable, then TS-STATS will work out a range of statistics which describe that single variable. If we specify two variables, then the module will also work out a range of additional statistics, assuming that we wish to explore the relationship between these two variables. The most common types of relationship which we may wish to explore are **correlation** and **regression**, both of which will be examined in more detail.

The entry screen for this module is almost identical to that of the preceding two modules and so we shall move straight to the analysis stage. We shall assume that we are using the MYSURVEY.TXT file yet again, but this time we are interested in examining the following continuous variables:

P_INCOME   Total parental income (in £1000s)

SALARY   Salary anticipated after graduation (in £1000s)

EXPLANATION OF THE OUTPUT

[First screen]

File: B:MYSURVEY.TXT	P_INCOME	SALARY
Measures of Central Tendency		
Mean	20.822	10.500
Median	17.000	10.000
Mode	10.000	15.000
Measures of Dispersion		
Minimum	7.000	6.000
Maximum	49.000	15.000
Range	42.000	9.000
First Quartile	11.000	7.000
Third Quartile	29.500	13.000
Semi-interquartile Range	18.500	6.000
Variance	129.446	9.523
Standard deviation [population]	11.377	3.086
Standard deviation [sample]	11.406	3.094
Standard Error of the Mean	0.813	0.220
Measures of Distribution Shape		
Skewness	0.777	0.013
Kurtosis	-0.567	-1.379

[Second Screen]

File: B:MYSURVEY.TXT	P_INCOME	SALARY
Numbers of Cases		
N	197	198
Missing Values	3	2
N (valid pairs)	195	
Summary Statistics		
x, y	4102	2079
Σx^2, y^2	110914	23715
x, y (adjusted: pair-wise deletion)	4075	2044
Σx^2, y^2 (adjusted: pair-wise deletion)	110545	23306
xy	48443	

Bi-variate Statistics

Correlation	r = 0.8290	t = 20.597	p = 0.0000
Regression	y (SALARY) = 5.767 + 0.226 * x (P_INCOME)		
T-Test (difference in means)	t = 12.261	D.F. = 224.54	p = 0.0000

This is another good illustration of the way in which a computer can generate a lot of statistics relatively easily, but the user needs some prior knowledge in order to interpret them. As this is a book concerned with the details of survey design and not with statistics as such, then it would not be appropriate to give a detailed description of each of these statistics in detail. However, some general guidance will be given about the kinds of output that TS-STATS generates and how it may be used.

Measures of central tendency

These statistics are different ways of measuring an average. The mean is identical with the arithmetic average whilst the median is the value that attaches to the central value (or average of the two central values) once the data has been arranged in order. The mode is the most frequently occurring value.

Measures of dispersion

These are measures which indicate the 'scatter' of the data – are the cases fairly well bunched up around the mean or are they scattered more evenly along the range? The simplest measure is the range (maximum–minimum). The quartiles embody the same philosophy as the median in that it is assumed that the data is split into four quarters rather than two halves once it has been arranged in order. The semi-interquartile range measures that half of the data that comes between the first and the third quartiles.

The variance is the average of the squared deviations of each data value from the mean, whilst the standard deviation, the most commonly used measure of dispersion, is the square root of this. Statistics textbooks tend to give two formulae for the standard deviation, one being appropriate for the whole **population** and one being a slight adjustment (a denominator of $n - 1$ instead of n) for the standard deviation of a **sample**.

The 'standard error of the mean' is a more specialized measure, utilized in statistical testing. We can use it in the process of **estimation** – once we have a sample mean, then we can be 95% confident that the 'true' population mean will lie within the range: sample mean $\pm$ 1.96 'standard errors of the mean'.

Measures of distribution shape

These are fairly specialized measures, included for the sake of complete-ness only. **Skewness** is a measure of whether the data contains cases that cluster towards the left (or low end) of the distribution in which case it is said to be positively skewed. Data which clusters towards the right-hand side (or top end) of the distribution is said to be negatively skewed. A value of zero indicates that the data has no skew at all.

Kurtosis is a measure of the extent to which the distribution has a fairly marked peak (higher values) or a fairly shallow peak (lower values).

Numbers of cases

In this section of the output, displayed on the second screen, the user is informed of the numbers of valid cases (N) as well as the missing values. The number of 'valid pairs' is also displayed – this figure tells us that number of pairs of data that are valid data, for if a figure in one column is a 'Missing Value' then the corresponding number in the other column will need to be excluded when correlation and regression data is being calculated.

Summary statistics

These statistics are of use if you are checking the results of a calculation by hand and wish to make a check on any of the following:

Sum of x	$(\sum x)$	Sum of x^2	$(\sum x^2)$
Sum of y	$(\sum y)$	Sum of y^2	$(\sum y^2)$
Sum of xy	$(\sum xy)$		

BI-VARIATE STATISTICS

The TS-STATS module assumes, if you have entered two variables, that you wish the bi-variate statistics to be calculated. The first variable which you entered should have been known as the **independent** variable (x) whilst the second variable for which you were prompted was the **dependent** variable (y). You may think of the term 'independent' variable as being roughly synonymous with 'cause', whilst the term 'dependent' variable may be seen as the effect. So if we are examining how two variables are related, say INCOME and FOOD, then we would make the assumption that the amount of food that you buy would be the **dependent variable** (y) as it 'depends' upon the amount of money that you earn – the **independent variable** (x).

The concepts of correlation and regression are important, so they will be elaborated in a little more detail.

Correlation

When we calculate a **correlation coefficient** (r), we are calculating how much two variables vary with each other. There will be some variables that vary directly with others – the more you have of one, the more you tend to have of the other, as the preceding example of INCOME and FOOD indicates. This will be known as a **positive** correlation. On the other hand, we can have circumstances in which, as one variable increases, so the other decreases. A good example might be that in a sample of school children, as length of legs increases, so the time taken to run 100 metres decreases. This is known as a **negative** correlation. We may also have a situation in which there is no association at all between the variables.

The strength of a correlation is measured by a correlation coefficient

(r) which takes any value between −1 (perfect negative correlation) and +1 (a perfect positive correlation) with 0 being the point of no correlation at all.

The following summary may be helpful:

    0.0 . . . ± 0.3   Weak association, or correlation
    ± 0.3 . . . ± 0.7 Moderate association, or correlation
    ± 0.7 . . . ± 1.0 High association, or correlation

One of the most important points to bear in mind in the interpretation of correlation coefficients is that **correlation does not imply causation**. The fact that two variables appear to vary with each other may be due to the fact that the association is entirely spurious, such as the case noted by an economist in which there was a very high association between the imports of strawberry jam from Bulgaria and the marriages solemnized by Methodist ministers in the 1970s! Sometimes, of course, it may be that variables that **appear** to be unrelated are in fact related to each indirectly via some variable that is affecting them both jointly. There **is** an association between storks and babies born in the southern states of the USA – such a relationship appears spurious but when another variable such as 'level of urbanization' is introduced, we can demonstrate that as the level of urbanization increases, so do the levels of both the stork and the human populations **coincidentally** increasing at about the same rate. Correlation coefficients need to be interpreted with a great deal of care. All that they actually measure are that two variables are varying directly with each other. The reasons **why** they are varying may be due to the fact that there is a causal relationship. Or it could be that the relationship is very indirect as in the 'storks and babies' case cited above, or indeed it may be entirely spurious. Although politicians are exceptionally prone to making causal connections between observed sets of data ('Labour governments cause inflation' whereas 'Conservative governments cause unemployment'), as social researchers we are obliged to be a lot more cautious. All that we can say is that there **may** be the **possibility** of a causal connection between two variables that are shown to be highly correlated but we cannot say that a **causal** relationship exists until a much fuller investigation has taken place.

Regression

When we have two sets of data and we suspect that they are related, then we may wish to use the data to try and predict the values of one variable given certain values for the other. The concept of regression is closely related to that of correlation but whereas correlation measures the degree to which the sets of data vary with each other, regression is a tool that we wish to use in order to attempt to predict new values.

To do this, we use a **regression equation** which always takes the form:

$$y = a + bx$$

where y is the symbol for the dependent variable whose value we wish to predict, x is any **given** value for the independent variable and a, b are constants. The a constant is called the 'intercept' and the b constant is called the slope of the line.

An example will make this clear. Let us suppose that we have a regression equation which links **FOOD** with **INCOME** – the variable **FOOD** is the amount spent by a family on food each week whilst **INCOME** is the amount of income they receive.

Now let us imagine that on the basis of past data, we have worked out the regression equation relating **FOOD** and **INCOME** and the actual formula is:

$$y = 2.5 + 0.2x$$

We wish to predict what a family with an income of £200 per week will spend on food. As the independent variable, x, takes a value of 200 then the equation becomes

$$y = 2.5 + 0.2(200) = 42.50$$

Regression equations tend to be used most in circumstances where the data lends itself easily to a mathematical treatment and where we already have a body of collected data that we can use to try to predict other values.

A more homely example will be used to conclude the discussion of regression. When you wake up in the morning, you probably switch on the light, making the assumption that the electricity authorities had generated enough electricity to supply your home as well as everybody else's. How much electricity does the company know it needs to generate? If it generates too little, then there will have to be power reductions or power cuts, whilst if it generates too much, then this will waste fuel and cut its profits. One major determinant of how much electricity to generate will depend upon the predicted temperature for the following day. Accordingly, the electricity utilities will have received weather forecasts the preceding day and will attempt to predict the likely demand for the following day by using a regression equation. If the weather is likely to drop below freezing, then it should be possible to forecast fairly accurately what the demand for electricity is likely to be.

You would use regression data from your survey data, therefore, primarily in order to make predictions or projections from your existing data about the values that might be taken by the dependent variable for any given level of the independent variable. Let us just recall the relevant section from the output shown previously:

Bi-variate Statistics
~~~~~~~~~~~~~~~~~~~~

Correlation   r = 0.8290   t = 20.597   p = 0.0000
Regression   y (SALARY) = 5.767 + 0.226 * x (P_INCOME)

This tells us that the data is quite highly correlated (r = 0.829). Also, if we wish to predict a graduate's salary from that of his/her parents' income, assuming that the parents have an income of 20 (= £20 000 per annum), then we would say:

y(SALARY) = 5.767 + 0.226(20) = 10.287 (£10 287 p.a.)

't'-tests

A statistical test of significance known as a 't'-test can be performed on the two sets of data to see if their means differ from each other significantly. On many occasions, this will be true by accident as one would have no reason to expect that the means should be similar. However, were one to select two variables that might be expected to have similar means, then the 't'-test will report significant differences. The critical figure to observe is the p-value (probability value) – any figure **less than** 0.05 indicates that there is only a 5% probability that the means differ as a result of chance factors alone, and therefore there is a corresponding 95% probability that the means differ as a result of non-chance factors operating. The interpretation of the 't' and 'p' statistics is discussed further in the following section.

HYPOTHESIS TESTING

In the preceding module TS-CROSS, we used the chi-square test when we wished to see if there was an association between two variables measured at the categorical level. In the same way, we can use a statistical test called a 't'-test to see if statistically significant differences exist within data that is measured at the continuous level.

Let us take the example of two variables – SEX and SALARY. SEX is obviously measured at the categorical level and can only take a value of 1 or 2 whilst SALARY is measured at the continuous level. What we wish to do is to 'cut' the data into two portions – the anticipated salary for women and the anticipated salary for men – and then see if a statistically significant difference exists between the two means.

When we have chosen our two variables SEX and SALARY and viewed the results, then we are presented with the following choices (the user input is underlined):

```
Perform a t-test of the variables        [Y]es      [N]o

It is necessary to divide the variable SEX
into two groups to perform the t-test

The Minimum of SEX is        1.000
The Maximum of SEX is        2.000

Minimum of Group 1      ?    1
Maximum of Group 1      ?    1

Name you wish to give to Group 1 [8 characters or less] Females

Minimum of Group 2           2
Maximum of Group 2           2

Name you wish to give to Group 2 [8 characters or less] Males
```

We can explain this dialogue as follows. The categorical variable, SEX, is being used to divide the data into two portions. As it happens, SEX only has two values 1 and 2 and hence both the minimum and the maximum values for the first group – Females – are a 1. Similarly, the values for Males are a 2. If we were to have a CLASS grouping rather than a SEX grouping then we might have wished to split the data into 'White collar' versus 'Blue collar' in which case the minimum and maximum values might have been 1–3 and 4–7 respectively.

Once we have given TS-STATS the information to split the continuous data into two groups and the names that we wish to give to these two groups, then the following analysis is performed:

Two sample test of SEX by SALARY				File: B:MYSURVEY.TXT	
SEX		N	MEAN	STDEV	SE MEAN
Group 1	Females	102	10.206	3.454	0.342
Group 2	Males	94	10.543	3.040	0.314

T-Test (difference in means) t = 0.726 D.F. = 193.60 p = 0.4689

Again, some of this data may not be meaningful until you have done a course in statistics. But the critical figure to look at is the 'p' figure which has to take a value of 0.05 or less in order for us to say that there is a statistically significant difference between the sexes. In general terms, the 't' figure needs to be in the region of approximately 2 or over but, in any case, TS-STATS works out the exact probability or 'p' figure that it needs from the 't' statistic and the degrees of freedom.

In this case, if we inspect the mean figures for SALARY, we can see by looking at the data that there does not appear to be much difference between the means (10.206 as against 10.543 (£1000s)). The 'p' figure of 0.4689 tells us that 46.89% of the time we would get these differences by chance alone. A statistician would conclude that there is **no** difference between what the different sexes expect to earn and would only change his/her mind when the 'p' value drops to 0.05 or below.

HISTOGRAMS

If you decide not to do a 't'-test, then TS-STATS offers you the choice of performing a HISTOGRAM of your data. This is a rough and ready diagrammatic representation of the data so that you can see what 'shape' the data has.

Having chosen this option, we are presented with the following dialogue (the user input is underlined):

```
Histogram of SALARY

Minimum of SALARY is    6.0    Histogram minimum?    1
Maximum of SALARY is   15.0    Histogram maximum?   16

No of classes in the histogram [2-20]?    16

Histogram of SALARY Anticipated Salary   File: B:MYSURVEY.TXT


CLASSES     COUNT      PERCENT
16.0          0          0.0%
15.0         28         14.1%    *****************************
14.0         18          9.1%    ******************
13.0         18          9.1%    ******************
12.0         19          9.6%    *******************
11.0         15          7.6%    ***************
10.0         19          9.6%    *******************
 9.0         16          8.1%    ****************
 8.0         15          7.6%    ***************
 7.0         26         13.1%    *************************
 6.0         24         12.1%    ************************
 5.0          0          0.0%
 4.0          0          0.0%
 3.0          0          0.0%
 2.0          0          0.0%
 1.0          0          0.0%
            --------    --------
Total        198        100.0%
Missing Cases  2
```

As you can see, the histogram analysis is not very sophisticated but does give a visual 'clue' as to the shape of the data. In this particular case, the data appears to be quite uniform.

TS-STATS does offer some control over the number of classes in which you have your data displayed. Owing to the very great variation in the way in which continuous data is displayed, it attempts to put the data into uniform categories, but the mathematical results of doing this may not be the categories that you expect. It is best to start at a value of 1 if you possibly can and to choose a number of classes that extend beyond the range of your data.

SCATTERGRAMS

Whereas histograms look at the distribution of one variable at a time, if you choose the SCATTERGRAM option you can observe how two variables vary with each other. An example is shown of **P_INCOME** and **SALARY**:

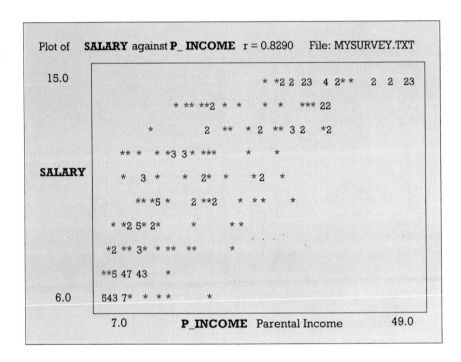

Notice how the first variable that you specify, the independent variable, forms the horizontal axis whilst the second variable, the dependent variable, forms the vertical axis. The asterisk represents the position of a single plotted case. When TS-STATS tries to plot more than one case in a single position, it specifies a number rather than an asterisk – hence a '3' indicates that three cases are plotted on to that particular point. In excess of nine cases, TS-STATS uses the 'X' symbol. Finally, as a bonus, the Pearson product moment correlation coefficient (explained on pp. 75–6) is calculated and displayed on the top line of the graph.

If you specify a categorical variable, the output may look rather strange as in the next example:

```
Plot of   SALARY against SEX        r = 0.0214   File: B:MYSURVEY.TXT

  15.0
           X                                               X

           X                                               8

           9                                               8

 SALARY    X                                               8

           7                                               7

           7                                               X

           9                                               7

           7                                               7

           X                                               X
   6.0     X                                               8

              1.0              SEX  Sex of Individual          2.0
```

This is actually absolutely normal because the variable of SEX can only take one of two values (1 or 2). Normally, of course, a scatter plot would be used with two continuous variables – the more closely the data appears to cluster around a line, the more highly correlated are the two variables. If the line slopes from bottom left to top right (like the slash '/'), then this is indicative of a positive correlation, whilst if it slopes from top left to bottom right (like '\'), this is indicative of a negative correlation. If you divide the graph mentally into four 'quadrants' and the data appears to be equally split between all four quadrants, then this is indicative of no relationship at all.

Remember also that the **absence** of a relationship between two variables might be much more significant to the researcher than the **presence** of a relationship. It is important not to assume that getting a high correlation is an indication of 'success' and a low correlation of 'failure'. The interpretation of the correlation coefficient depends upon the background expectations of the researcher in much the same way as the hypothesis tests that were examined earlier.

Using the TURBOSTATS editing modules

8

We have already examined the three principal analysis modules supplied with TURBOSTATS. Now, we are going to turn our attention to the ways in which we can both enter and edit our datafiles.

In Chapter 3 we saw how we could prepare the datafiles and the labels files for TURBOSTATS. If you are used to using a word-processor or a text editor that can write in 'plain ASCII' mode, that is without any special formatting characters, then you may prefer to use these familiar tools for preparing your files. However, a facility is provided within TURBOSTATS to generate these files, called TS-ENTRY. In this chapter, we shall also examine a further module, TS-CASES, which allows us to create 'sub-files' containing only particular types of cases should we need a more detailed analysis.

CREATING YOUR DATA AND LABEL FILES WITH TS-ENTRY

When you first enter the module, you are presented with the following choices. It is assumed that you are going to create your variable names first as this then acts as a prompt for the labels that you are going to create as well as the data.

```
TS-ENTRY              TURBOSTATS              (c) M. C. Hart [1992]
~~~~~~~~~           ~~~~~~~~~~~~            ~~~~~~~~~~~~~~~~~~~~

   MENU
   ~~~~

   [1]   Enter Variable Names
   [2]   Enter Variable Labels
   [3]   Enter numerical data
   [X]   To EXIT

   Choice ?  1
```

Having chosen the first option, then the following screen is presented. As usual, the user entry is underlined. We assume here a small survey with three variables only.

```
Enter variable names [max 10 characters]. You may modify entries later.

Number of variables ? 3
   1 SEX        2 SMOKER      3 DRIVER

Data Entry Complete      Modify any entries [Y]es [N]o?  N
```

Having composed the variable names, we now choose to enter the labels. When this item is chosen from the menu, we have the following information screen.

TS-ENTRY   **TURBOSTATS**   **(c) M. C. Hart [1992]**
~~~~~~~~~   ~~~~~~~~~~~~   ~~~~~~~~~~~~~~~~~~~~~

Writing Variable Labels
~~~~~~~~~~~~~~~~~~~~~~~

Each variable may have ONE variable label and up to NINE value labels
associated with it.

For each variable, you will be prompted to supply the following
information

● The VARIABLE label associated with the variable

● The number of VALUE LABELS

● The actual value labels themselves

Each VARIABLE label may be up to 25 characters long and each VALUE
label may be up to 15 characters long. However, shorter VALUE labels
are superior as these are often truncated in the output tables,
particularly of TS-CROSS [Cross-tabulation tables]

Press ENTER to proceed ..

Having pressed ENTER, we would proceed to fill in the first of the
screens. The process cycles through each of the variable names we have
chosen.

Variable		SEX
Variable label	?	Sex of Individual
No of VALUE labels	?	2
Label 1 is:		Female
Label 2 is:		Male

On completion, we are prompted for a filename, complete with drive
and extension, in which the labels file should be saved.

```
TS-ENTRY              TURBOSTATS              (c) M. C. Hart [1992]
~~~~~~~~~              ~~~~~~~~~~~~~           ~~~~~~~~~~~~~~~~~~~~~
Specify filename for labels

Include both the DRIVE and the EXTENSION e.g. a:myfile.txt
leaving no spaces..

Filename ? d:demo.txt


d:demo.txt now written to disk

Press ENTER to continue
```

Having returned automatically to the TS-ENTRY sub-menu, we are now ready to start entering some data. One sample screen is shown below.

```
RECORD 1

SEX        1      SMOKER    2      DRIVER    1

Record 1 complete. Are all entries correct      [Y]es  [N]o  Y

Another record      [Y]es  [N]o  Y
```

If you continue to answer **Y** then you will prompted for all of the data until it is completed. As soon as you enter **N**, the module assumes that you have finished your data entry, prompts you to supply a filename as in the case of the labels file and then gives the opportunity to exit.

OTHER WAYS TO ENTER DATA

The TS-ENTRY module is a 'slow but sure' way in which to enter data. If you are already a fairly experienced computer user, then there are faster ways in which you can create both your datafiles and labels files.

Using a text editor

A text editor is by far the quickest way to enter the data, but it does not give you the security associated with TS-ENTRY. On the other hand, it does allow you to 'scan' all of your data quickly and to make alterations rapidly as you go along. The author uses a text editor to prepare

datafiles and a small, public domain, WordStar-compatible text editor
(TE.EXE) is supplied along with the system. More details can be found
in Chapter 9.

Using a database

The advantage of using a database for data entry is that you can specify
the field names as your variable names and then use this as a prompt for
your data. For example, here is a dBASE III database being used as an
entry system. First the database is created with the 'CREATE filename'
command, in this case:

CREATE DEMO

```
C:demo.dbf                          Bytes remaining:    3997
                                    Fields defined:        3

     field name    type      width    dec
     =============================
  1  SEX           Char/text    1
  2  SMOKER        Char/text    1
  3  DRIVER        Char/text    1
  4                Char/text
```

Once the database is created, then the data is entered as follows:

```
            Record No.        1
            SEX           1
            SMOKER        2
            DRIVER        1
```

Finally the whole database can be copied to a text file with the
command (from the dBASE prompt):

COPY TO D:DATAFILE.TXT DELIMITED

Using a spreadsheet

Yet another way of entering data is by using a spreadsheet. This has the
advantage of having all of the data in view but without the benefit of
variables names/labels. An example is shown from **TC.EXE** – the small
spreadsheet supplied with the TURBOSTATS system. Only a portion of
the spreadsheet is shown here.

TurboCalc – Customized for **MICROSTATS/TURBOSTATS** Memory: 253659

	A	B	C	D	E	F	G	H	I
1	1	2	1						
2	2	1	2						
3	1	2	1						
4									
5									
6									
19									

C4 Empty   *C:\TS92\DP0

F2-Save **F3**-Load **F7**-Formula **F8**-AutoCalc **F9**-Recalc **F10**-Menu
Ins-Block **Alt-X**-Exit

Having entered the data, one would print it to a file instead of the printer with the following sequence of commands. The user input is underlined.

F10 Spreadsheets Print   (Name of file:) demofile.txt
Compress the printing? N   Print the borders? N

The file demofile.txt will then be written for you. Remember, though, that this is an **ASCII** text file, in which form data can be imported into TURBOSTATS. However, like other spreadsheets TC saves its data in its own particular format and if you wished to retrieve your original data from TC, you would have to have saved it first with the **Alt-F2** (Save As) command.

We therefore have at least four ways in which datafiles can be prepared. Each has its particular advantages and disadvantages. For a small survey, then the use of a text editor is hard to better. Once the survey gets larger and more complex, you may need to consider using a database, if only for its data entry facilities.

USING THE TS-CASES MODULE

When we were using the TS-CROSS module, we noted that there were times when we might be interested in having smaller sections of files that we could use for more detailed analysis. For example, if we were conducting a public opinion poll survey of voting intentions, we might think that women are more likely to vote right and men are more likely to vote left. However, we know that voting is influenced by education, so is voting behaviour more influenced by our sex or by our level of education?

To attempt to answer this type of question, we really need to split the datafile into two sections. In the language of social research, we need to hold one variable 'constant' whilst allowing the others to vary. Let us imagine that we have a variable HIGH_ED which is a simple category determining whether or not our respondents had experienced any form of full-time higher education. We can then use this variable to create two datafiles – one containing the 'Highly educated' and the other containing the 'Not highly educated'. We then examine the relationship between SEX and VOTING in both of our two datafiles. If there appears to be the same proportion of men and women voting right/left irrespective of education, then we can conclude that the impact of higher education on voting is slight or non-existent. If, on the other hand, there appear to be marked differences in the pattern of voting between the sexes depending on prior experience of higher education, then we may be able to conclude that it is this experience, rather than gender, which is influencing voting intentions.

This type of analysis is known as **multivariate analysis**, to distinguish it from the **bi-variate analysis** in which we were examining only two variables at a time. Multivariate analysis is, by its very nature, complex and many investigators do not venture far beyond examining the relationships between two variables whilst holding constant the level of a third. In practice, we can perform fairly sophisticated analyses using this technique. If we wanted to be able to give more causal 'weights' to the effects of different factors, operating either independently or in conjunction with each other, then we need to use the tools of factor analysis and multivariate regression to be found in more sophisticated statistical packages such as SPSS or Statgraphics.

To create the 'sub-files' that we need for analysis, the TS-CASES module presents us with the following dialogue, after the opening screen. The user input is underlined.

Specify the MINIMUM and MAXIMUM values of the variable CLASS to be used in selecting your cases

Minimum ?   <u>1</u>
Maximum ?   <u>2</u>

Do you wish the values between   1.0 and   2.0
to be INCLUDED in, or EXCLUDED from, your output file?

Specify [I]nclude [E]xclude <u>I</u>

Specify complete name of output file including Drive and Extension
e.g. a:myfile.txt

Name of output file? <u>d:demofile.txt</u>

Now reading from B:MYSURVEY.TXT and writing to D:DEMOFILE.TXT

The module then informs the user how many cases have been written to the output file you have specified and gives you the option of choosing another variable, another file or quitting the module. In the example we have used above, we have specified the variable of CLASS and chosen the first two categories ('Professional' and 'Intermediate') to create a file containing only 'White collar workers'. We can then repeat the process to create a file containing only 'Blue collar workers' and then be in a position to engage in the type of more specialized analysis to which we have already referred.

The TURBOSTATS utility programs 9

In this chapter, we shall be examining how we can use several utility programs supplied with the TURBOSTATS system. In many cases, the use of these utilities is integrated, or designed to work closely with the rest of the system, but they are also 'stand-alone' utilities that can be used in their own right.

WHAT HAPPENS WHEN YOU RUN THE TURBOSTATS SYSTEM

The user will know by now that once the system is correctly installed, it is brought into use by the simple command **TS**. However, it is instructive to know a little about 'what goes under the bonnet' and so some explanation will be given of the ways in which the various components of TURBOSTATS link together. When you type TS you are activating a **batch file** which performs the following sequence of operations.

- A specialized file MARK.COM is run to keep a note of the memory allocation.
- The screen clears and the **SNAP** package is run (used to capture screen outputs, about which more in a moment). This program is known as a 'Terminate-and-Stay-Resident' (TSR) program – it waits in the background until called into play.
- Then a screen of information is displayed by running a program named TS-OPEN. The user is given the opportunity of allowing a few bars from the opera 'Don Giovanni' by Mozart to play or not. You have the opportunity to turn this off if you like.
- The main menu program, TS-MENU, is then run from which the user can select by number any one of the more specialized programs such as TS-FREQ1, TS-CROSS or TS-STATS.

- This program converts the areas of memory which have been used to store the screen images into files. Finally, the SNAP program is removed from memory and the system restored to the condition in which the TURBOSTATS system found it.

THE INDIVIDUAL TURBOSTATS MODULES

Although TURBOSTATS is intended to be run as an integrated system, each of the principal modules is a 'stand-alone' program which can be run from the DOS command line merely by specifying its name. It is for this reason that when you use the individual modules you are always prompted for the name of your datafile and your labels file. Whilst you may to wish to use a module by itself from the DOS command line, you will not be able to copy an individual module on to another disk and use it from there. Each module looks for authentication information and if this is not found, the package refuses to run.

USING SNAP TO CAPTURE YOUR SCREEN OUTPUT

The SNAP program allows the user to take 'snapshots' of the screen in much the same way as one would if using a camera. These 'snapshots' are stored in memory and are only available to the user once the TURBOSTATS session has ended.

To capture a screen is very simple. The **PrtSc** key, normally used to dump the screen contents to the printer, is diverted by the program to act as a SNAP key. Once it is pressed, you will hear a beep and the caption SNAPSHOT.01 appears towards the top right-hand side of the screen. This caption will **not** subsequently appear on your output. To prevent you taking multiple snapshots inadvertently by pressing the **PrtSc** key longer than intended, a slight delay is built in after each snapshot – so that you have to wait up to 2 seconds before you can take another. As you take more snapshots, then the extension will be incremented by one until you reach your limit, which is SNAPSHOT.30. It is good practice to keep a brief note of the contents of each snapshot so that you know which to retain and which to discard, in much the same way as you would with snapshots taken with a camera.

USING DEVELOP TO DEVELOP YOUR SNAPSHOTS

As we have just explained, the TURBOSTATS batch file **TS-BAT** automatically activates the DEVELOP program as you exit from the system. Until the DEVELOP program is run, the snapshots stay captured in the computer's memory but are unavailable to the user.

The DEVELOP program takes the areas of memory devoted to the snapshots and converts them into files: SNAPSHOT.01 and so on up to the limit of SNAPSHOT.30. The files are saved on to whichever disk you specify when you run the program DEVELOP.EXE via the batch file, TS. If you run the modules independently of the batch file, then you need to run DEVELOP.EXE and specify the drive where you wish to save the snapshots at the end of your session.

The DEVELOP.EXE program allows you to specify

- The drive for the location of your snapshots.
- A default filename other than SNAPSHOT to help avoid overwriting other files (e.g. you could choose SNAPFILE).
- Whether or not you want a form-feed on each snapshot.
- A one-line description of each snapshot in a .LOG file.

An important point to remember about DEVELOP is that it does **not** check to see whether you already have some SNAPSHOT files on your disk. If in one session you had laboriously created 30 snapshots and saved them on disk, then DEVELOP quite happily overwrites them with whatever it saves in a subsequent session. The solution to this lies in the user renaming the SNAPSHOT files as something more memorable. For example, we could use the command from DOS:

ren snapshot.* session1.*

and all of the snapshot files will now have the name of session1 (to remind you that these were the files from your **first** session) but with the same extension numbers.

It is a good idea to view your snapshot files regularly and either rename them or delete them so that your data disk does not become too cluttered with them. Each file takes approximately 2000 bytes of storage space.

These snapshot files are pure 'text' files and are not saved in a specialized graphics format. They are therefore available for you to read into whichever word-processing package you are using to produce your final written report. In WordStar or the WordStar clones, you would typically use the command ^**KR** (^ means 'hold down the **Control** key on the keyboard') in order to read a file into the document you are writing. As the files are text files, they can be edited to fit the shape of the page or your overall layout in whichever way you like. For example, snapshots were used extensively in the preparation of this book to supply readers with the types of screens that could be expected when TURBOSTATS is used. But as the screens that were snapped could be up to 80 characters wide, they were edited to make them fit more easily with the rest of the text.

USING THE LINE-DRAWING CHARACTERS CONVERSION ROUTINES

It is evident that some of the screen output involves the line-drawing characters to be found in 'high ASCII', i.e. codes from 128 to 255. Some printers and indeed some word-processors have difficulty in interpreting these characters and therefore some conversion routines are supplied should you be having difficulty in getting your output to appear in the way which you would like.

A file is supplied called BOXCONVT. If you run it with no parameters (filenames supplied to it) then you get the following set of instructions:

BOXCONVT   by Mike Hart

Converts ASCII single-line drawing characters
into printable ASCII characters ..

Vertical line characters	:	|
Horizontal line characters	:	−
Intersection characters	:	+
Bar-chart characters	:	*

SYNTAX: BOXCONVT oldfile.txt newfile.txt

You should find the 'high ASCII' characters are replaced by others which can be guaranteed to work on any printer, as shown in the following brief table:

```
Crosstabulation of SEX    Sex of Individual      File:
             By CLASS  Social Class              B:MYSURVEY.TXT
```

CLASS >	Profes sional 1	Interm ediate 2	Skille d Manu 3	Semi-s killed 4	Unskil led Ma 5	Pensio ners 6	Not cl assifi 7	ROW TOTAL
SEX								
Male 1	16	12	10	16	22	2	20	98
[Row %]	16.3	12.2	10.2	16.3	22.4	2.0	20.4	51.6%
[Col %]	57.1	75.0	41.7	50.0	47.8	12.5	71.4	
Female 2	12	4	14	16	24	14	8	92
[Row %]	13.0	4.3	15.2	17.4	26.1	15.2	8.7	48.4%
[Col %]	42.9	25.0	58.3	50.0	52.2	87.5	28.6	
TOTAL	28	16	24	32	46	16	28	190
	14.7%	8.4%	12.6%	16.8%	24.2%	8.4%	14.7%	100.0%

```
Valid cases = 190   Missing = 10
```

If you wish to automate the process even further then simply typing in the command CONVERT will activate a batch file which looks for any files named SNAPSHOT.0?, converts the characters in them to 'printable' characters and then copies them over to a new set of files entitled SNAPFILE.0?.You could well find a use for these utilities quite apart from the SNAPSHOT files created by the TURBOSTATS system.

THE SORTED DIRECTORY UTILITY PROGRAM

This little program (SD.COM) is a public domain Sorted Directory program. It is available from the main TURBOSTATS menu and, as its name implies, it gives you a directory sorted alphabetically by default. It is therefore useful for navigating your way around your data disks if you have forgotten the names of some of your datafiles or labels files. If you run SD as a stand-alone program from DOS, you can specify various options, detailed for you on the top line of the program and most of which are self-explanatory. For example, SD /S sorts by size, SD /X sorts by extension and so on.

THE TE TEXT EDITOR

Another utility supplied with the TURBOSTATS system is the **TE.EXE** text editor. This is a stand-alone program which works with generally the same basic command set as WordStar. A summary of the command set can be seen by pressing the **F1** key from within the program.

The complete TE suite of programs consists of the following:

TE.EXE	Complete program
TE.DOC	Author's documentation for the program
TE_NOTES.TXT	Guide to text editors and to TE, written by M. C. Hart

Readers are referred to my own notes, TE_NOTES.TXT, in the first instance – you can read this using TE itself by using the command TE TE_NOTES.TXT. Abandon the file by the command ^KQ followed by **Y** for Yes when prompted.

It is possible to alter both datafiles and labels files from within the TURBOSTATS system itself, should you wish to make a minor change. In order to do this, you would specify Option 7 ('Load a program of your own choice') from the Main Menu. When prompted, you will have to specify the full name as known to DOS which in this case is **TE.EXE**. When you are prompted for a parameter, specify the name of the datafile or labels file that you wish to modify. The following bit of 'dialogue' may make this clear:

Specify full name of program to run e.g. a:aseasy.com

Name of program to run   ?   te.exe

Parameter if any   ?   b:labels.txt

The complete command summary, as supplied by the package author, is reprinted here for convenience:

TEXT EDITOR 2.5 COMMAND SUMMARY

TE [Path] [FileName]	c-Ctrl s-Shft a-Alt

File

c-KD, c-KQ, F4	Save file and quit editor
c-KE, F2	Save and/or load another file

Cursor Movement

c-S, Left	Char left	c-QS, Home	Line begin
c-D, Rt	Char right	c-QD, End	Line end
c-A, c-Left	Prev word	c-QE, c-Home	Screen top
c-F, c-Rt	Next word	c-QX, c-End	Screen bottom
c-E, Up	Prev line	c-QR, c-PgUp	File start
c-X, Dn	Next line	c-QC, c-PgDn	File end
c-W	Scroll up	c-QB	To block start
c-Z	Scroll down	c-QK	To block end
c-R, PgUp	Up 23 lines	Tab	Next word, prev line
c-C, PgDn	Dn 23 lines	s-Tab	Prev word, prev line
c-Q4	To specified line	c-Kn	Set line mark n=0-3
c-QP	Dn page ten lines	c-Qn	To line mark n=0-3

Insert/Delete

c-V, Ins	Insert/Replace	c-H, BkSp	Delete left char
Entr	Split/Insert line	c-G, Del	Del char/join line
c-N, F9	Insert line	c-T	Del next word
c-Y, F10	Delete line	c-QY	Del to end line

Block

c-KB, F7	Mark block start	c-KC	Copy block
c-KK, F8	Mark block end	c-KY	Delete block
c-KH	Hide/display block	c-KV	Move block
c-KI	Block right 1 char	c-KR	Read block from disk
c-KU	Block left 1 char	c-KW	Write block to disk

Miscellaneous

F1	Display summary of Text Editor commands
c-QF	Find phrase (1–31 chars) in file or block
c-QA	Find/replace phrase (1–31 chars) in file or block
c-KP, F5	Print file or block to LPT1, LPT2, or LPT3
a-Xa-Ya-Z	ASCII code XYZ = 32–255 on keypad
c-P	Then a-Xa-Y on keypad for ASCII XY = 1–31
c-KS, F3	Temp return to DOS. Back to TE: EXIT
c-QM	Set left/right margins, page length
c-B	Format paragraph to left/right margins

The major points of contrast with WordStar are noted below.

TE FEATURES – DIFFERENCES WITH WORDSTAR

Most WordStar commands will work with **TE** but here are some differences.

^QM   Sets both left and right margins, page length.

^KS   Exits to DOS (so that you can count the words in a document, or do 'housekeeping' on files). (Think of the **S** as **S**ystem, not as **S**ave.)

^KE   Allows a temporary save (after prompts) and then resumes an edit of the same file. (Think of the **E** as **TE**mporary or as **E**dit.)

Tab   Will move the cursor to a position underneath the next word in the preceding line. (Shift–Tab moves the cursor to the preceding word.)

THE TC SPREADSHEET

Another 'free' utility, supplied with the TURBOSTATS system, is the **TC** (TurboCalc) spreadsheet program. This program was distributed by the software house Borland as a public domain utility, primarily so that programmers could get used to the facilities offered by their Turbo Pascal compilers.

Some brief documentation has been supplied by the author and the program itself has its limitations. When you run the program, you also need to specify a format file to go with it which will indicate the number of decimal places to which you require your output to be formatted. The dp0 file is probably the one that you would use most often and therefore you would specify:

TC dp0

The author would suggest that you use the package more as an aid to data entry rather than a serious 'spreadsheet' because some functions that you would expect, like replication, are a little difficult to use. However, some users have found it very valuable when entering large sets of data as they can keep a visual check on all of the data entered to date and can easily make modifications using the spreadsheet cursor. It is provided here 'as is' and it is free. Again, you could call this from Option 7 of the Main Menu if you so wish.

The dp? files should be created first by copying the tc? files as follows:

COPY tc? dp?

Then run TC-FILES.BAT which will make your dp? files 'system' and 'hidden' in which form they can be used by TC.EXE but not saved and overwritten.

To save a file in **TC** format, you would then use the command **Alt-F2** (Save As), in which format you could retrieve it for further use. Were you to write an ASCII datafile in order to export data to TURBOSTATS, then this file **cannot** then be loaded back into **TC**.

THE PIECHART PROGRAM

This is a small and stand-alone utility which you may find useful. It is best run apart from the TURBOSTATS system as the SNAP program cannot capture its graphics output. When running the program, specify the labels and values according to the instructions and then print off the resulting graph with **PrtSc**. Note that you will have to run the program GRAPHICS supplied with DOS first before this graph will print out correctly. It will do this in landscape mode but it is fairly slow and not very sophisticated. You probably already use a spreadsheet that will give you a better pie chart than this one, but the program is free.

A TEMPORARY EXIT TO DOS

Finally, if you know the exact location of your COMMAND.COM file (which may be on your root directory or in a sub-directory called SYSTEM or MSDOS) then you can also call this via Option 7. This loads a 'secondary command processor' from which you can perform what-ever operations you like, such as renaming and deleting files and other such 'housekeeping', before you return to the TURBOSTATS system with the EXIT command. Evidently, this is for the somewhat more experienced DOS user, but with a little experimentation you may well find ways in which you can make your system even more versatile.

UTILITIES AVAILABLE FROM THE OPENING MENU

Although not displayed on the Opening Menu, the following utilities are available and can be loaded and run by pressing the appropriate key:

\ Temporary return to DOS (type **EXIT** to return to TURBOSTATS)

! Run **MICROSTATS** (public domain version statistics program)

\# Run **TC.EXE** (TurboCalc spreadsheet program)

& Run **TE.EXE** (Text Editor public domain editor)

Writing the research report 10

Considering the importance of the research report as the culmination of the research activity, it is surprising how few books on social survey methods devote much attention to this topic. Research that is not 'written up' is tantamount to research not done.

THE 'SHAPE' OF THE RESEARCH REPORT

If you have conducted research on behalf of some sponsors, then it may be worth while discussing the overall shape of the report with your sponsors before you set pen to paper. In particular, you might wish to be concerned with the overall length, especially if this affects the reprographic costs associated with circulating the report to large numbers of interested recipients. Your sponsors may well wish to have a report presented in their own 'house style' and may have other examples of reports as a general guide for you to follow. However, it is true to say that the researcher generally has considerable discretion over the way in which the report is to be written up and presented.

THE MAJOR SECTIONS

These can be summarized fairly easily:

Purpose   what you set out to do
Methods   how you went about doing it
Results   what you found out
Discussion   how you evaluate your results, particularly in comparison with the other literature
Conclusions   what follows from your results

Recommendations   what you think ought to be done
Appendices   examples of the questionnaire (if used) etc.

The first four of these headings are unproblematic. However, the Conclusions and Recommendations sections could be omitted or written only in a tentative manner, depending upon the brief that you were initially given when the research was commissioned. If it was considered to be your job to 'find out' whilst it was for your sponsors to take the overall decisions based upon your findings, then your own views may not be welcome. On the other hand, your sponsors may well be interested in your own conclusions and recommendations. To avoid misunderstandings that can occur, these points are best clarified before the report is finally written and presented.

WHAT GOES INTO A RESEARCH REPORT

In general terms, you should always give as much detail as is necessary for other people to evaluate the quality of your work and, if necessary, replicate it. As well as your substantive findings, your report should also contain details of the methods that you employed and an assessment of the quality of the data that you were able to gather. What follows is a type of 'checklist' of features that you should normally think of including at one place or another in the completed document. Some of the items would best be left to an appendix whilst others should evidently feature more prominently.

For whom was the research done?

Full details should be given of who commissioned and funded the research. It is conventional to give acknowledgements to individuals and organizations who have given generously of their time, money and facilities to support the whole research operation. If the research is not sponsored as such, then some background details or context in which the research took place are appropriate, including reference to other published work in the area.

The object of the research

This might sound self-evident, but it is not unknown for research to start off with particular aims in mind and then for these to change in the course of the investigation. You should give a clear statement of the reasons for conducting the survey and the reasons why the results are needed or may be of some significance.

The timing and duration of the research

Details should be supplied of the time period over which the data was collected. Do not forget to put a date on the cover of the final report, so that the readers can be informed whether the data can be regarded as relatively up to date.

Who was studied?

This is a description of the subjects of the study, not just the sample which happened to be drawn. For example, if we were studying students on a sandwich degree course, we might want to detail our subjects as being on the first, second and final year of a four-year sandwich degree course in a provincial university. There are occasions when it is necessary to preserve the anonymity of the group of respondents in which case one would give suitable pseudonyms such as 'Midtown', a town in central England.

Sampling details

It is very important to supply details of the sample selected and particularly the figures that relate to the initial sample size, the non-response rate, the refusal rate and finally the 'net' sample size. If the response rate was very low and/or the refusal rate was very high, then this needs reporting honestly with perhaps a brief discussion of the extent to which the overall results may have been affected. Some might feel tempted to miss out these details altogether, but the diligent reader will spot this. Neglecting to give the sample details tends to indicate either a lack of competence or something that you might wish to hide.

Methods of data collection

The ways in which you gathered the data are of great interest. For example, was the data collected by a mailed questionnaire or did interviewing take place? The reader does not want a methodological treatise at this point but sufficient details to gain a good overall impression of the methods used and adequacy of the methods to 'tap' the research problem under investigation. Problems encountered in data collection should be reported honestly – research is often a messy rather than a straightforward business and it is not uncommon for events to occur, outside the control of the investigator, which can affect the overall result. This is particularly true of items getting lost in the post! The investigator should always strive to report results and methods also as honestly as possible, even though this may be painful at times.

Who undertook the research?

If you had utilized interviewers to collect the data, then some information should be given regarding their recruitment, selection and training. Very often, the researcher is his/her own data gatherer, in which case this too should be reported.

The research instruments used

Throughout this book, it has been assumed that the data has been collected by a questionnaire, either mailed or administered. However, whichever method of data collection was used, the research report should contain the appropriate details, usually in an appendix. Then it would be possible for the reader to assess the quality of the questions asked and possibly also to form an assessment of whether any of them tended to suggest a particular answer – the so-called 'leading questions'. Knowing that your questionnaire is going to form part of the overall document is yet another reason why considerable pains should be taken to perfect the questionnaire. When printed in its entirety, it also enables other researchers to replicate some or all of your own questions in subsequent research which greatly aids the comparability of research results over time.

The results

There is a great temptation to say that the results might 'speak for themselves' but unfortunately they do not – even the selection of results to write up involves the discretion and judgement of the researcher. As a practical point, it is probably worth while considering printing a list of the frequency distributions for all of the categorical variables and of the statistics for all of the continuous variables. In the latter case, you could edit out some of the more obscure statistics that were not likely to be of much interest.

The case of cross-tabulations is more difficult to judge. There is always the temptation, particularly if using a package like SPSS on a mainframe computer, to go on what is sometimes described as a 'fishing expedition'. This means instructing the computer to cross-tabulate each categorical variable with perhaps each other variable, whilst holding other variables constant for good measure. It is not an exaggeration to say that hundreds of pages of cross-tabulations could be generated in this way.

At the analysis stage, the investigator should have a clear idea of precisely what cross-tabulations are needed. At the writing-up stage, one would then print the cross-tabulations that were deemed to be of particular interest and indicate that no other cross-tabulations showed significant differences. Here, the reader has to place a lot of faith in the integrity of the researcher. The researcher has to be completely ethical in what is published and what is not.

Embarrassing findings can sometimes be hidden by the expedient of not reporting the relevant tables. In many ways, the selection of which cross-tabulations to publish in the report and which to ignore is one of the hardest tasks in social research. The important point is that the data has been analysed at one time by the researcher and interested parties can always contact him/her for further details should they wish to pursue a particular point.

Commentary on the results

It is incumbent on the researcher to add some words of explanation to a table of figures by way of interpretation. This should be as factual as possible, the intention being to 'round out' the overall picture given by the statistical data. The readers can always look at the data for themselves and attempt an evaluation of whether the conclusions drawn are justified. It is worth re-emphasizing at this point that the researcher should be very wary of drawing any conclusions from data sets that are very small and in particular not report percentages when the figures are too small to justify such an analysis. It is better to report the figures accurately and to state that the number of cases (n) is too small for percentages to be meaningful.

Comparison of results with the literature

In order to set your own findings into context, comparisons with similar surveys should be reported where possible. The research project probably started off with a literature search and therefore the researcher should have been aware of similar work in the field. Exact comparisons are not always possible with surveys that have been designed in

different ways and which have been conducted with different populations at different times. None the less, an attempt to relate your findings
to those of other researchers makes a research report more interesting
and relevant.

Implications or recommendations

Up to this point, the researcher will have been operating in a purely
factual rather than an evaluative mode. Depending upon the brief that
was originally given to the researcher, it is generally legitimate to draw
more evaluative conclusions from the data. One might wish to suggest
policy changes, or new methods of working depending upon what is
revealed in one's data. Many reports end with a plea for further research
in the area, or at least an indication of the new directions that might be
taken if the funding and researcher's time allow it.

CONSTRUCTING THE REPORT – READING IN YOUR 'SNAPSHOTS'

In Chapter 9, there was a detailed examination of the ways in which you
could view the contents of your analysis in the various TURBOSTATS
modules and take a 'snapshot' of the relevant screens. These snapshots
are then turned into text files and as such are available to be incorporated, as required, into your final research report.

The ways in which you read files into your document vary from
word-processor to word-processor. In the WordStar family, you would
read in a file with the $^\wedge$KR command whereas you would use $^\wedge$F5 in
WordPerfect. Consult your manual if necessary to find the ways to read
in or import files.

Once the text file is read into your word-processor or text editor, you
can edit it in whichever way you like. It might be that you have to
'squeeze' the material a little to make it fit within your current margins.
Or there may be superfluous data which you can selectively delete. If
you find you have made a disaster of your attempts to edit the file, you
can always delete the offending lines from your text and read it in again.

There are only two problems that are likely to occur in practice. The
first is that your imported text might overflow your current margins.
The solution is to select a left-hand margin of 1 and a right-hand margin
of 80 before you read in the text, then edit to fit in with your desired
margins and finally reinstate your preferred margins.

A second problem is concerned with the 'box-drawing characters'
which might not produce the desired output in your word-processor

and/or your printer. If this is the case, then use the conversion routines detailed in Chapter 9 **before** you read in the file.

An important point to bear in mind when you are importing tables of figures is that you would not want a page break to occur in the middle of a table. You therefore need to know how to keep all of your output together on the same page. One way is to put a 'new page' character immediately before the table which ensures that your table starts off on a new page. You may find that this can be a 'fiddly' process but it is, regrettably, unavoidable. The author prefers to use a text editor rather than a word-processor to produce reports containing many tables of figures, because in this way the writer has complete discretion over exactly where the page break can occur.

As well as incorporating individual snapshot files into your text, you may wish to produce an appendix with the total number of screens (and therefore snapshots) as a continuous stream of text. You would get the output in a presentable form by taking the following steps:

- Let us assume that you have six snapshot files. You can 'collate' them into one long file with the following command from DOS:

  copy snapshot.01+snapshot.02+snapshot.03+snapshot.04
  +snapshot.05+snapshot.06 totals.doc

  If you were certain that your snapshots were stored on disk in the correct order (check with the DIR command) then this can be shortened to:

  copy snapshot.*   totals.doc

- TOTALS.DOC now contains all of your snapshots in one continuous stream of text. Typically, each snapshot file will take up to 24 lines of text, so you can only guarantee getting two of them on to a page. Now read TOTALS.DOC into your word-processor or text editor and settle on a consistent format. For example, you may wish to have two blank lines at the top of every page as a header and five lines between your two snapshots. Put a new page symbol, such as ^L, at the end of the second snapshot and repeat the process for the rest of the file.

- The new page symbol can be generated in different ways. In WordStar you can try the 'dot' command **.PA**, but you can also try the ASCII page feed symbol ^L which can be entered directly by trying the sequence ^PL.

THE STYLE AND PRESENTATION OF THE REPORT

When writing a research report, the researcher always has to be thinking 'Who is going to read this?' The question is not academic because it can profoundly influence not only the overall contents of the report but also the language in which it is expressed.

If you are writing a report for a limited circulation of technically informed individuals or as an academic paper in a journal, then you would be expected to produce a report complete with technical details. When reporting the results of a significance test, for example, you could report the 't' and the 'p' figures obtained but you should not need to explain what these terms mean.

A report for the general public on the other hand should keep these technical details to the absolute minimum. If necessary, the more technical details can be published in an appendix for those who wish to consult them there.

The choice of language and style is not easy. One needs to write in a simple but informative style without attempting to be amusing or patronizing. Often you may feel that you are being forced to oversimplify issues. If, on the other hand, the language becomes too turgid or complex then you are not conveying what you intend. This advice is certainly easier to give than it is to follow consistently.

Bear in mind also the house style of the organization to which the report is to be presented. Some organizations like a summary and recommendations to be printed **before** the main body of the report is presented, whilst others feel that any recommendations should only come **after** the analysis. It is always a good idea to let a sponsor have an initial draft of the report to allow some influence over the choice of presentational style and so on. The researcher has to be careful to preserve integrity and not allow a sponsor to indicate approval/disapproval of sections of the report before it is officially handed over. In the author's experience, sponsors are often pleased to look at a copy of the draft report and usually make helpful suggestions.

The importance of good layout is hard to overemphasize. The report should make good use of 'white space', i.e. blank lines between paragraphs and even between the paragraph heading and the body of the text. The way in which a document appears may be as important as the words themselves. The researcher should strive for a consistent, clear and readable format which the reader finds easy to follow.

As producers of word-processed documents will know, there are some important technical points to aid the overall presentation. A 'binding margin' allows the document to be bound without obscuring the text. A document which is line-spaced at 1½ lines (4 lines per inch) is usually easier to read but will increase the overall page length.

It is often forgotten that once the report has been printed and the pages numbered, a final important task remains. That is to create a **contents page** so that the readers can find particular sections of the report when they need to. A front cover with some graphics output can generate a professional appearance even before the report has been read. Finally, the type of printer used adds to the impression of quality, the ideal being to get the document printed on a laser printer if this is at all possible.

Trouble shooting **11**

The TURBOSTATS system has been used and tested extensively for several years to conduct both surveys and student projects. It has been designed to be 'user-friendly' and performs its job well given the limitations inherent in a small application package. However, a series of hints will be given to help you to conduct your analysis smoothly and avoid any potential difficulties.

ARE YOUR DATAFILES AND LABELS FILES ACCURATE?

Having selected the module you wish to use and then requested both the datafiles and the labels files, TURBOSTATS will look for these files and then attempt to read them. If the system then appears to 'freeze' or to 'lock up', it is because it is attempting to read a badly constructed file and cannot get any further. This is evidently frustrating and the user has to re-boot the system in order to gain control.

The TURBOSTATS system reads in data one line at a time and looks for the carriage return/line feed pair of bytes at the end of each line to read in data one line at a time. (Do not be concerned if you do not understand these technical details.) The user could, by accident, have concluded a line without this carriage return/line feed pair or might have included a space after the last character in the line which will again cause problems.

If you have a word-processor or a text editor which shows the position of your carriage returns, then check for the source of the error if your file 'hangs' the computer in this manner. If you have access to the VDE text editor, it becomes very easy to make the carriage returns visible by using the ^OB toggle – the first use activates the toggle whilst the second deactivates it. If not, you can always use the

SHOW_CR.COM utility file provided by the author on the distribution disk which will hunt for the position of all the carriage returns in your file and turn them into (visible) backward-pointing chevron symbols («). The instructions are shown below – they are shown on screen when you type in SHOW_CR with no filenames to process.

Show_CR   by Mike Hart

Looks for the carriage return byte (ASCII 13) at the end of each line and replaces it with a 'back chevron' («) character.

Syntax: SHOW_CR oldfile.ext newfile.ext

Use the LIST utility with your newly created file to view the result.

As you can see, you supply the name of your deviant file and a new filename and **SHOW_CR** creates the new file which you can then view using the **LIST** program. If any carriage returns are missing or you have spaces immediately before them, then this will be visible and you can make the necessary corrections to your original file with your own word-processor. The use of the batch file, **CR.BAT**, is recommended at this point as it automates the process for you, creating a second file in which you can view the end-of-line character. Remember that this second file is only for error-correcting purposes – it cannot be used for data input. You use it to identify possible problems in your original file which you should then correct with your usual word-processor/text editor.

PROBLEMS WITH THE LABELS FILE

You should attempt to ensure that your labels file **always** follows the examples provided in Chapter 3. In particular, make sure that the variable name is in block capital letters and that you do not have a space between the variable name and its associated label or a space before the carriage return. You should also ensure that you have your quotation marks (') around each variable and variable name, which should be a maximum of 25 characters long:

    "SEX","Sex of student"«
    "SEX","Female"«
    "SEX","Male"«
    etc.

The labels file here is shown with the carriage returns made visible (using the same display as **SHOW_CR**). The variable names should always be spelled in the same way. Make sure that you have enough labels to fit all the values likely to be found in your data but do not have more than nine to avoid problems.

PROBLEMS WITH THE DATAFILE

Here, it is a good idea to make your data 'rectangular' (making all of the columns line up with each other) as indicated in the following fragment of a file:

```
1,1000,2«
2,   0,1«
1, 700,4«
etc.
```

The carriage returns are shown explicitly in the example above. If the data is made rectangular, then it becomes much easier to check it by eye if you suspect that you have any errors. As in the case of the labels files, make sure that you do not have any trailing spaces after the end of your last number before the carriage return. TURBOSTATS can cope with a blank line at the beginning or at the end of your datafile but it is a good idea to avoid these if you can. You can use the delete line facility in the WordStar family (^Y) to delete any extra lines that may have crept in at the bottom of your file. As the datafile and the labels file have to work closely with each other, then any discrepancies between the two will show up, particularly when you use the TS-FREQ1 module. If you find that your labels from the **following** variable are creeping into your display, it means that you have more values in your datafile than you have matching labels. If you have excess 'labels' for values that do not occur then these will be ignored, but a problem is likely to occur if you have values without labels that will match up with them.

CAPTURING THE SCREEN OUTPUT WITH SNAP

The major problems that are likely to occur here are that the user forgets to specify the destination drive when the snapshots are developed by the program DEVELOP.EXE. It is good practice to keep one disk devoted just to your datafiles and labels files as well as your 'snapshots'. When you exit the system, take care to note that the procedure activated by DEVELOP is actually writing your snapshots to disk as you intended. This process is often easier to observe if your data disk is a floppy because you will generally see evidence of disk activity when the drive light is activated during the 'write' operation. It is good practice to train yourself to be vigilant that this 'write' operation is proceeding satisfactorily. Make sure also that you have sufficient room on your floppy for the snapshot files to be stored.

A second problem is that the user may overwrite a first set of snapshot files with the results of a second session. Remember that each session starts numbering the snapshot files from .01 and does not check your disk to see if any have already been stored. So, again, it is good practice to rename your snapshot files to something more memorable as soon as you have finished that particular editing session. In this way you not only have a set of filenames that are more descriptive but you will also avoid the 'overwriting' problem. If you are not sure how to rename your files, then consult your MS-DOS manual.

Make sure that you know how to read the snapshot files into your word-processed report. In the WordStar family, you would use the command ^KR to read in a file, but check how you do it in your usual word-processor.

THE OUTPUT IS SPLIT OVER TWO PAGES IN THE REPORT

Whenever a big table is incorporated in to a report, there is always the danger of a page break occurring in the wrong place. Try putting the page break symbol (which looks like the biological symbol) into your document immediately before the table with the command ^PL. You may also need to edit the output so that it fits within the current margins. See Chapter 10 for more details.

ABORTING MODULES

When a module aborts, you are returned quickly and apparently without warning to the Opening Menu. If a problem has occurred, then the individual module prints a warning but control is passed swiftly back to the calling menu program before you have much of a chance to do anything about it.

The occasions when a module aborts are hopefully extremely rare. The most typical circumstance is one in which the package has been asked to do an impossible calculation, such as dividing zero by zero in order to calculate a percentage, for example. The TS-CROSS program seemed prone to this problem at one time until it was possible to program around it. If you find that this problem re-occurs then one solution might be to attempt the cross-tab the other way around, or to try one option at a time until you find the one that appears to be causing the problem. Running the module from DOS rather than through the menu may also give some hint of the problem.

PROBLEMS WITH LINE-DRAWING CHARACTERS

Given the variety of word- and text-processing packages as well as printers used to display the results, then problems may be experienced in getting the line-drawing characters used in TS-CROSS to display correctly. The SPSS system, for example, allows you to specify the use of the '-', '|' and '+' characters to draw its boxes. The solution lies in knowing the characteristics of your own word-processing package and printer. If you cannot get these characters to import or to print correctly, then use the **BOXCONVT** utility which will convert all the line-drawing characters into 'low ASCII' characters that can be read and printed without difficulty. Chapter 9 gives fuller details.

TRUNCATED-VALUE LABELS

The advice given in Chapter 4 is that the value labels you write should be a maximum of 15 characters long. However, your variable labels can actually be longer so long as you are aware that they are likely to be 'truncated', i.e. cut off beyond a certain limit in certain forms of output. This is most likely to occur in the TS-CROSS module when there is only a limited amount of space available for the column labels. The label will be truncated to 12 characters and then will be 'bent around' to provide two lines of six characters which is the total cell width available. The TS-CROSS row labels will be truncated after the 15th character. However, if you are going to produce frequency distributions only, then you can write value labels that are longer – up to 20 characters – before they will be truncated to fit the output.

The advice therefore is to keep your value labels as short as practicable. If you had two labels such as the following:

"DRINKING","Admits drinking often"
"DRINKING","Admits drinking sometimes"

then both your labels will be truncated to read 'Admits drinki' for each of the columns, which is going to be confusing. The solution is to have a variable label which explains the output, such as

"DRINKING","Admits to drinking .."

to which the value labels can then be "Often","Sometimes","Rarely", etc.

If possible, the variable label should reflect the original question in your questionnaire as closely as possible, although you may be forced to make some pragmatic compromises when you compose your labels.

THE ANALYSIS OF MULTIPLE CHOICE QUESTIONS

In common with other survey analysis packages, TURBOSTATS cannot cope with multiple choice questions – the type in which several answers may be ticked in a list. This type of question may be best avoided if you intend to analyse the results statistically but if it is unavoidable, then a sensible method of analysis would be to treat the question **as though it were** a series of individual questions, each with a 'Yes' or 'No' answer. These answers can then be fed into TS-FREQ1 so that you can get the numbers and percentages of people who picked that particular item. You might then need to compose your own little summary table of the responses.

THERE ARE TOO MANY CATEGORIES IN THE DATA

As we have already seen when we were examining cross-tabulations, it is possible to have so many categories in the data that the number of responses in each 'cell' shrinks to very low numbers when it comes to the analysis stage. The solution here lies both in careful design and perhaps some re-coding at the analysis stage. A moment's reflection will reveal that if we have a sample of 30 and we are inviting one of ten responses, then the average number for each cell will be three and in all probability many cells will be vacant. We therefore need, at the design stage, to ensure that the number of categories is broadly consistent with the total number of responses that we hope to collect. The criterion is to make sure that we have enough in each 'cell' to arrive at some sensible conclusions and this evidently calls for some judgement and experience. Even so, there will be occasions when your cell sizes shrink very low. If, at the design stage, you have thought carefully about the ways in which the categories could be collapsed if necessary, then this eases problems at the analysis stage. One good practice is always to have two 'positive' categories (one strongly so, one mildly so) and two equivalent 'negative' categories. The responses can then be 'collapsed' if necessary into two broad categories of 'Positive' and 'Negative'. An illustration may help here. Imagine we are collecting 'Attitudes to smoking in public places' and have the categories:

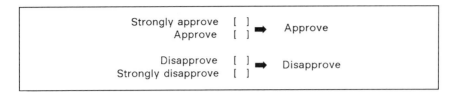

Assuming that these were numbered 1, 2, 3 and 4 we could then recode numbers 1, 2 into a 1 and 3, 4 into a 2 in a new datafile. Having created a slightly amended labels file, we could then analyse the data in two categories ('Approval' and 'Disapproval') rather than in four.

PROBLEMS IN INTERPRETING THE STATISTICAL OUTPUT

Whilst analysis packages can do all of the hard work in calculating the statistics for you, the one thing that they cannot do is to supply you with an understanding of what the output actually means. One needs to develop a certain amount of skill and experience in 'reading' the results of a table, for example to see what information is conveyed.

The problem is greatest when it comes to interpreting both the χ^2 and 't'-test statistics. However, the key comes in understanding the nature of the **probability** figure (the 'p' figure) which the relevant modules always work out for you.

The whole of statistical testing rests upon the assumption that an event (e.g. a difference between two means) has occurred either because there is a **real** difference between the two samples that are being compared or because such differences that we observe are due to chance factors, such as drawing a rather biased sample. If we were conducting a survey of public opinion, for example, we might be very unlucky and collect a sample of only Conservative voters. The probability figure indicates the likelihood that we are getting the result by the operation of chance factors alone. Statisticians normally make the assumption that what is regarded as statistically significant is a p-value equal to or less than 5% (or 0.05). This means that there is only a 5% chance that the results we observe could have arisen by accident and therefore a corresponding 95% chance that the differences we observe in our data are **real** differences.

Once we are attuned to this statistical way of thinking, then all we need to do is to train ourselves to observe the probability figures and say to ourselves that

$p = 0.05$ or less   **Significant differences**
$p = 0.06–1.00$ **No significant differences**

A FINAL WORD ON TROUBLE SHOOTING

The analysis and writing of a research report calls for many skills to be exercised simultaneously. You will need to have a working knowledge of the MS-DOS operating system to ensure that your files are kept in good order. Remember that the TURBOSTATS system is essentially a tool and there are some things that it cannot do, or cannot do well. For example, no attempt has been made to write graphics routines as so many of these already exist in high-quality shareware packages. As well as using TURBOSTATS, you will also need to know at least the rudiments of a word-processing package so that you can produce your final report.

If all else fails, then it might be better to have a few neatly hand-drawn charts or diagrams if you cannot get the computer pack-ages(s) to do what you want.

If you experience problems, then adopting an experimental attitude may help you to identify the source of the problem. Let us imagine that, having examined your datafiles and labels files, they still seem to be 'hanging' the system. In this case, try making a copy of the first ten cases or so of your datafile and see if the problem persists. If not, then you know that the problem resides somewhere between case 11 and the end of your datafile. Adopt the same philosophy with your labels files – if necessary, use the SHOW_CR program. If you are a more experienced DOS user, then you can locate troublesome non-printing characters in your files by using DEBUG or by using the Alt-H (Hex Dump) mode of the LIST utility provided on the distribution disk.

It may also be worth while to study a 'dump' of your files on paper to see if you can find the problem. Often, errors are much easier to 'see' on paper than they are on screen.

It is reported that managers of software houses who are responsible for offering advice and help-line support to users of their products often have a large sign over their desks with the motto RTSMF! This is reported to be an acronym for

'Read The S—— Manual First!'

and it is true that many apparent problems can be resolved by a careful reading of the instructions relevant to each program. A careful and systematic approach to your data files and labels files can pay dividends in the long run. Do not be too anxious to get your first analysis up and running even though this can be done fairly quickly. A consistent approach to missing values, for example coding them all as a zero, is often beneficial and makes them easy to find and check using the 'Find' facilities in your text editor. Knowing the various facilities offered by your text editor will also pay many dividends in the long run.

Appendix A
Interfacing with other software

The TURBOSTATS system works on 'pure' datafiles, that is those that can be produced on any word-processor or text editor. A public domain text editor, **TE.EXE**, is supplied together with the rest of the system to help you to produce these files if necessary. As TURBOSTATS is designed both to read and to write pure ASCII datafiles rather than files in any particular format, it is quite easy to interface with other products. Two are particularly worthy of mention and are very widely available: **dBASE** (formerly produced by Ashton-Tate, now by Borland) and the Lotus 1-2-3 spreadsheet clone, **ASEASYAS**.

dBASE III

The dBASE package is particularly good in that it is very easy to create a database and then use this as an 'input screen'. The advantage of using dBASE when entering large volumes of data is that by default the system will beep when one field is full and the cursor is about to enter another. From the user's point of view, this means that large volumes of data can be entered quickly without looking at the dBASE entry screen. If users are reading the data from the input document, then they can rely upon an 'auditory cue' to know that they are now entering data into the next field. Once one is sensitized to the fact that a beep does not signify an error but is an indication of satisfactory progress, then very rapid data entry is possible because it is generally not necessary to complete an entry with the ENTER key and this therefore minimizes keystrokes.

In the dBASE sampler disk, the user is limited to 30 records but at least the disk is free! After every 30 records, the user can write a datafile with a command such as

COPY TO data_1.txt DELIMITED

and a text file can then be written. The database can then be 'zapped', i.e. cleared of records whilst keeping the structure intact, and another 30 records can then be entered. The next set of records could be written to another datafile such as data_2.txt and so on *ad infinitum*. The datafiles can then be stitched together into one complete datafile from the MS-DOS command line with a command such as the following:

COPY DATA_?.TXT   complete.txt

dBASE also comes complete with its own miniature text editor, activated with

MODIFY COMMAND ‹textfile.txt›

where ‹textfile.txt› is the name of your datafile. The dBASE editor has a limit of 5000 characters which would process a 100 cases long 20 item questionnaire. For longer files, you specify the text editor of your choice by putting a line such as:

TEDIT=TE.EXE

in the configuration file (**CONFIG.DB**). The example illustrates the ways in which you can specify the TE text editor.

The author would recommend dBASE heartily if only for its data entry and word-processing capacities.

ASEASYAS

This is a very widely available clone of the Lotus 1-2-3 spreadsheet. The author would recommend it if you wanted more sophisticated graphing facilities than are provided by TURBOSTATS.

The ASEASYAS package will draw bar charts, pie charts and plots with the ability to label the axes and the graph itself. You can save the output of TS-FREQ1 and import the results directly into ASEASYAS with the /File Directory Import Values command if you wish. From here you highlight the relevant data and labels columns as inputs for your bar chart or pie chart.

OTHER UTILITIES PROVIDED ON THE DISTRIBUTION DISK

VALIDTXT.EXE will take two text files and compare them for discrepancies byte by byte, reporting any discrepancies that it finds. This utility is particularly useful if you have prepared your datafile twice, once as the 'original' and then once again in order to perform a 'validation' (see pp. 8–9 for further details). Once a discrepancy is found, you will have to turn to your original source document for the correct value and then ascertain whether the error has occurred in the 'original' or in the 'validation' file. Ensure that the two files agree with each other with the correct value(s) and then repeat the process until no more errors are found.

CRCK4.COM is a 'Cyclical Redundancy Checking' program that computes a specialized 'checksum' (similar to a signature) for any particular file. This program is used by the **CR.BAT** file as a final check to ensure that the two files, the original and the validation copy, are completely identical. Activate this batch file with the command:

CR original.txt validate.txt

Appendix B
Good PC management

If you are using the TURBOSTATS package, it is assumed that you already have some experience of the basics of the MS-DOS operating system. Here, though, are a few words of advice concerning your disks and how to take care of them.

Your TURBOSTATS distribution disk should be copied and the original put away in a safe place, before you start any work at all. You can then install TURBOSTATS on your copied disk, keeping the original in case of loss or disasters.

As the distribution disk is already quite full, it will **not** be suitable for storing your datafiles. If you are using TURBOSTATS on a dual floppy system with TURBOSTATS on Drive A, then you should be putting your datafiles on to your floppy in Drive B. As the cost of floppies is getting cheaper all the time, it is a good idea to have several newly formatted floppies available before you start a work session.

If TURBOSTATS is installed on a hard disk system, make sure you are saving your data on your floppy and **not** on the hard disk where it is capable of being overwritten in subsequent sessions. As a reminder, you specify where you wish your snapshots to be written when they are developed by the DEVLOP.EXE program on exit from the system. From here you use the LIST facility to view them, or a text editor to modify them. Rename them immediately so that you know what they are and keep careful (hand-written) records of your snapshots.

Once you have datafiles and labels files that are complete and working (they appear to load correctly) then immediately take backup copies of them. Remember that the data on the floppies is a lot more valuable than the storage medium itself. Clear out old backup files (those with an extension of .BAK) to maximize the space on your floppy. And delete files that you are certain you no longer need in order to reduce the clutter.

As TURBOSTATS produces pure text files, these are easy to print out even without access to a word-processor. The command

COPY datafile.txt PRN

from the MS-DOS command line will print out the file ‹datafile.txt› for you on the printer, assuming it is connected and on-line.

Appendix C
Further reading

This book is intended to be a quick and practical guide to survey design and analysis but is **not** intended to be definitive or exhaustive. It is best used in conjunction with other texts which can give you a more detailed picture of particular aspects of research design. As it is necessary to have some knowledge of statistics, then a selection of what the author considers to be good, modern introductions to the subject are also included.

SOCIAL RESEARCH METHODS

Moser, C. and Kalton, G. (1971) *Survey Methods in Social Investigation*, Heinemann, London.

This book is regarded by some as 'the bible' of how to design and conduct surveys. It is definitive but somewhat dated now.

de Vaus, D.A. (1991) *Surveys in Social Research*, 3rd edn, UCL Press, London.

This treatment integrates statistics with survey design. It is up to date and definitive but fairly long. It certainly repays detailed study and contains very sound theoretical and methodological advice. However, you need several hours of intensive study before you could actually put this book to use in conducting and analysing a survey, so it is not a book where time is of the essence.

Reid, N.G. and Boore, J.R.P. (1987) *Research Methods and Statistics in Health Care*, Edward Arnold, London.

This is short, readable and written at an elementary level. Although its brevity might be commendable, the treatment of some of the issues is understandably scanty.

Bell, J. (1987) *Doing Your Research Project*, Open University Press, Milton Keynes.

A very useful guide for the first-time researcher, but the section on statistical analysis is very small.

STATISTICS

Curwin, J. and Slater, R. (1991) *Quantitative Methods for Business Decisions*, Chapman & Hall, London.

A modern textbook widely used on business studies and related courses. The book includes a software package **(MICROSTATS)** which helps take some of the tedium out of the calculations.
   A previous version of **MICROSTATS**, written by the author, is available 'free' on the TURBOSTATS distribution disk **(MS.EXE)**. The documentation for this program is contained in a self-extracting file, named **MS3MAN.EXE**. As there is insufficient space on the distribution disk for this documentation to be stored in an uncompressed format, users are advised to 'unpack' it on to another floppy with the command **MS3MAN B:** (where **B:** might be a floppy which contains sufficient space for the expanded file **MS3MAN.DOC** which is 65,570 bytes long).

Graham, A. (1990) *Investigating Statistics*, Hodder & Stoughton, London.

An excellent, conceptual and non-numerical introduction to statistical ideas written at the sixth form/first year of higher education level. This book provides an excellent 'first read' for those who have not been exposed to statistical concepts before and require a non-mathematical treatment.

Reid, S. (1987) *Working with Statistics*, Polity Press, Cambridge.

This is another introductory book which is gentle but introduces the reader well to the numerical methods needed.

Anderson, A.J.B. (1989) *Interpreting Data*, Chapman & Hall, London.

This book is intended for the first-year, undergraduate, market and contains useful chapters on topics such as demography and the sources of published statistics which are not often found in books of this type.

Hannagan, T. (1990) *The Effective Use of Statistics*, Macmillan, Basing-stoke.

This book is deceptively titled because there is as much material on collecting and displaying information as there is on statistical analysis. The work is sub-titled 'A Practical Guide for Managers' but it is worth consulting by all first-time researchers, whether managers or not. There is a useful appendix also ('Basic Maths for Managers') to serve as revision.

Denscombe, M. (1992) *An Introduction to Questionnaire Design*, Leicester Business School, De Montfort University, Leicester.

A brief but authoritative guide to questionnaire design complete with an example and a practical assignment.

Appendix D
Installation routines

The TURBOSTATS system needs an installation routine before its modules will run. Attempting to run a module before the installation routine has been activated will result in the package aborting and a 'Naughty! Illegal copy' message being flashed at you.

IMPORTANT! Before you start any installation procedure, make a backup copy of your disk using the DISKCOPY command from DOS. Put your original away in a safe place and then work ONLY from your copy.

TO INSTALL TURBOSTATS ON A HARD DISK

1. Create a sub-directory with the command
   MD \TS
   or any other sub-directory name of your choice.
2. Change to that sub-directory with the command
   CD \TS
3. Copy all of the files over from your distribution disk with the command
   COPY A:*.* [or B:*.*]
4. Run the package by typing the name of the batch file
   TS
   The package will automatically install itself the first time it is run.

TO INSTALL TURBOSTATS ON YOUR FLOPPY DISK

Run the package by typing the name of the batch file
   TS
The package will automatically install itself the first time it is run.

TO DEINSTALL THE TURBOSTATS SYSTEM

Run the program UNINSTAL before you delete files from a sub-directory.

TO INSTALL AN INDIVIDUAL MODULE ON A FLOPPY DISK

Copy the file TS-START.COM to your floppy as well as the individual modules required. **You MUST copy TS-START.COM over to your floppy BEFORE you install the full system as the program is designed to work on occasion only.**

Remember that the MARK.COM, SNAP.EXE, DEVELOP.EXE and TSR.COM files may need copying as well if you wish to activate the SNAP system. Remember to run MARK and then SNAP before activating the module and then DEVELOP and RELEASE after it to 'develop' your snapshots.

Appendix E
TURBOSTATS capacities

NUMBER OF CASES

TS-FREQ1 and **TS-CROSS**	10 000 cases
TS-STATS	3000 cases

NUMBER OF VARIABLES

For technical reasons concerned with the length of the input line, your datafile should contain lines not greater than 254 characters. Remembering that a position is occupied by each delimiter, then TURBOSTATS can accommodate

127 variables of length **1** (e.g. 1,2,3)
 84 variables of length **2** (e.g. 10,12,14)
 62 variables of length **3** (e.g. 123,456,6.7)

If you have a large data set, then consider splitting your whole project into two or more datafiles, ensuring that in each file you keep together those variables that you wish to cross-tabulate or to correlate.

NUMBER OF VARIABLE/VALUE LABELS

TS–FREQ1, TS–CROSS, TS–CASES	600 lines of text
TS–STATS	500 lines of text
TS–ENTRY	200 lines of text

SPECIAL CASES

If you need to exceed the number of cases or the number of variable/value labels then apply to the author for a 'custom-made' module.

Appendix F
Files on the TURBOSTATS distribution disk

BOXCONV2	**COM**	:	One of the box conversion programs
BOXCONVT	**COM**	:	The box conversion program
CHOOSE	**COM**	:	Used to get user responses in the **TS** batch file
CONVERT	**BAT**	:	Conversion routines for line-drawing characters
CONVERT1	**BAT**	:	A batch file called by **CONVERT.BAT**
CONVERT2	**BAT**	:	A batch file called by **CONVERT1.BAT**
CR	**BAT**	:	A batch file which runs the **SHOW_CR.BAT** program
CRC	**BAT**	:	Runs the **CRCK4.COM** checksum program (see below)
CRCK4	**COM**	:	Performs a CRC (Cyclical Redundancy Check) on a file
DEVELOP	**EXE**	:	This program 'develops' your snapshots
ID	**COM**	:	Gives your TURBOSTATS distribution disk ID number
LABELS	**TXT**	:	A sample labels file
LIST	**COM**	:	Public domain listing program
MARK	**COM**	:	Marks the position in memory of **SNAP**
MOD_ATTR	**COM**	:	Modifies the file attributes (used in **TC_FILES.BAT**)
MS	**EXE**	:	Public domain version of **MICROSTATS**
MS3MAN	**EXE**	:	Self-extracting documentation file (specify drive)
MYSURVEY	**TXT**	:	Sample datafile
PIECHART	**EXE**	:	A graphics program to draw pie charts

PUTXY	COM	:	Used to get user input in the **TS** batch file
RAMFREE	COM	:	Used to check that memory has been reallocated
RELEASE	EXE	:	Restores memory to its rightful condition
SD	COM	:	Public domain 'Sorted Directory' program
SHOW_CR	COM	:	Creates a file showing carriage returns as '«'
SNAP	EXE	:	A 'terminate-and-stay resident' snapshot program
TC	EXE	:	The free TurboCalc spreadsheet program
TC_FILES	BAT	:	Program to convert DP? files into 'system' files
TC0		:	TurboCalc formatting file: 0 decimal places
TC1		:	TurboCalc formatting file: 1 decimal place
TC2		:	TurboCalc formatting file: 2 decimal places
TC3		:	TurboCalc formatting file: 3 decimal places
TC_NOTES	TXT	:	Some documentation for TurboCalc
TE	DOC	:	Public domain text editor – documentation
TE	EXE	:	Public domain text editor
TE_NOTES	TXT	:	Mike Hart's notes on text editors (and **TE**)
TS	BAT	:	The principal **TS** calling program
TS-CASES	EXE	:	**TS-CASES** used to select particular subsets
TS-CROSS	EXE	:	The **CROSS-TABULATION** program
TS-ENTRY	EXE	:	The **DATA** and **LABEL ENTRY** program
TS-FREQ1	EXE	:	The **FREQUENCY DISTRIBUTION** program
TS-MENU	EXE	:	The principal **MENU** program
TS-OPEN	COM	:	The 'Preliminary Information' screen display
TS-START	COM	:	An installation routine (activated in **TS.BAT**)
TS-STATS	EXE	:	The **STATISTICS** program
TSINST-D	COM	:	Installation program for Drive D:
TSINSTAL	COM	:	Installation program for Drive C:
TSR	COM	:	Part of the memory management and restore system
UNINSTAL	COM	:	Program to uninstall the system
VALIDTXT	EXE	:	Validating program for two text files

Appendix G
Sample questionnaire

Reproduced by kind permission of the 'Leicester Environment City' campaign team and Ms Leticia Gaeta Gonzalez.

POINTS OF PARTICULAR INTEREST

(a) Instructions are repeated at the top of each page.

(b) Coding boxes and variable names are clearly shown on the right.

(c) Questions tend to be divided into two 'favourable' and two 'unfavourable' responses for ease of collapse into two categories if necessary.

(d) The initial letter conveys the essential information concerning the aims of the investigation and the question of confidentiality. Note the use of incentives to maximize the response rate.

(e) Finally, there is a promise that the results will be made available. The name and contact number of the researcher is given in case of any queries that might arise.

Environment City

Leicester Environment City Trust Limited
3rd Floor, Town Hall, Leicester LE1 6BF
Tel: 0533 554244   Fax: 0533 555726
Registered Charity No.1006604

3 February 1992

Environment City is a voluntary organisation working for a better environment as well as improving the quality of life for the people in Leicester.

This can only be done with the participation of all members of the community. Your team plays a very important role in making Leicester a cleaner, more attractive city in which to live.

Environment City is undertaking a research study to see how you and members of your team feel about your work and about the attitudes of the public towards you.

The research is <u>strictly anonymous</u> i.e. you <u>do not</u> have to state your name.

Please complete the attached questionnaire and return it to the same place where you collected it by Wednesday 5th February. When giving it back, please ask the person in charge for a ticket which gives you the opportunity to win a *"Colin the Caterpillar"* *T-Shirt.* The number of the lucky winners will be given next Thursday 6 February.

Thank you for your co-operation; please keep the biro provided.

Should you want more information on Environment City, please contact me.

Leticia Gaeta
Research Officer

LEICESTER ENVIRONMENT CITY
~~~~~~~~~~~~~~~~~~~~~~~~~~
CLEANSING DEPT. QUESTIONNAIRE
~~~~~~~~~~~~~~~~~~~~~~~~~~~~

L E I C E S T E R

Environment City

For office use only.

Please put a tick [✓] in ONE box only ...

1.	How long have you been working in your present job?			EMPLOY
	• Less than a year	[1]	[ ]	
	• 1 – 4 years	[2]	[ ]	
	• 5 – 9 years	[3]	[ ]	
	• 10 years or more	[4]	[ ]	

2.	How many hours do you work per week?			HOURS
	• 39 hours or less	[1]	[ ]	
	• 40 – 49 hours	[2]	[ ]	
	• 50 – 59 hours	[3]	[ ]	
	• 60 hours or more	[4]	[ ]	

3.	Which of these statements describes best what you feel about your job?			FEELINGS
	• Very enthusiastic	[1]	[ ]	
	• Quite enthusiastic	[2]	[ ]	
	• Not very enthusiastic	[3]	[ ]	
	• Not at all enthusiastic	[4]	[ ]	

4.	What team do you work for?			TEAM
	• Street sweeping vehicles	[1]	[ ]	
	• Street cleaners	[2]	[ ]	
	• Utility crew	[3]	[ ]	
	• Mobile team	[4]	[ ]	
	• Spare pool	[5]	[ ]	
	• Other (please state)	[6]	[ ]	
	....			

5.	Would you say that, to get the job done on time, there is:			PRESSURE
	• A lot of pressure	[1]	[ ]	
	• Some pressure	[2]	[ ]	
	• Not much pressure	[3]	[ ]	
	• No pressure at all	[4]	[ ]	

6.	Would you say that the amount of work is:			AMOUNT
	• Very high	[1]	[ ]	
	• Quite high	[2]	[ ]	
	• Not very high	[3]	[ ]	
	• Not at all high	[4]	[ ]	

	For office use only.
Please put a tick [✓] in ONE box only ...	

7. Would you change your job if you were offered:
- Much better pay but more work   [1]   [ ]
- Less heavy work for the same pay   [2]   [ ]
- Work with a different group of people   [3]   [ ]
- Other reason   [4]   [ ]
- None of these   [5]   [ ]

CHANGE

8. Which of the following is most important in your job?
- Contact with the public   [1]   [ ]
- The hours of work   [2]   [ ]
- Your fellow workers   [3]   [ ]
- Keeping Leicester clean   [4]   [ ]

IMPORT

9. Does your supervisor treat everybody in the group:
- Very fairly   [1]   [ ]
- Quite fairly   [2]   [ ]
- Not very fairly   [3]   [ ]
- Not at all fairly   [4]   [ ]

SUPERVR

10. Do you have a say in the decisions that affect you in your job?
- All of the time   [1]   [ ]
- Sometimes   [2]   [ ]
- Rarely   [3]   [ ]
- Never   [4]   [ ]

DECISION

11. Would you say that your 'take-home' pay was:
- Very good   [1]   [ ]
- Quite good   [2]   [ ]
- Not very good   [3]   [ ]
- Not at all good   [4]   [ ]

PAY

12. Have you lived in Leicester/Leicestershire for:
- Less than 10 years   [1]   [ ]
- 10 – 19 years   [2]   [ ]
- 20 – 29 years   [3]   [ ]
- 30 years or more   [4]   [ ]

LIVED

13. Would you say that Leicester/Leicestershire was:
- A very good place to live in   [1]   [ ]
- Quite a good place to live in   [2]   [ ]
- Not a good place to live in   [3]   [ ]
- Not at all a good place to live in   [4]   [ ]

FEELINGS

	For office use only.
Please put a tick [✓] in ONE box only ...	

14. What area of the city do you work in?
(Please write below e.g. Highfields, Knighton)

AREA_WK

☐

15. What are your feelings about working in that area?
  - Very much like it   [1]   [ ]
  - Quite like it   [2]   [ ]
  - Quite dislike it   [3]   [ ]
  - Do not like it at all   [4]   [ ]

AREA_FL

☐

16. Do you find the people in that area of the city:
  - Very friendly   [1]   [ ]
  - Quite friendly   [2]   [ ]
  - Not very friendly   [3]   [ ]
  - Not at all friendly   [4]   [ ]

AREA_FR

☐

17. How do you think the public view your job?
  - Very important   [1]   [ ]
  - Quite important   [2]   [ ]
  - Not very important   [3]   [ ]
  - Not at all important   [4]   [ ]

PUB_VIEW

☐

18. Would you say that the quality of service given
to the public by your team is:
  - Very high   [1]   [ ]
  - Quite high   [2]   [ ]
  - Not very high   [3]   [ ]
  - Not at all high   [4]   [ ]

QUALITY

☐

19. Do members of the public (including property
owners) co-operate when asked:
  - All of the time   [1]   [ ]
  - Sometimes   [2]   [ ]
  - Very occasionally   [3]   [ ]
  - Never   [4]   [ ]

PUB_COOP

☐

20. Do members of the public make the effort to keep
places in the city clean by putting litter in bins:
  - All of the time   [1]   [ ]
  - Sometimes   [2]   [ ]
  - Very occasionally   [3]   [ ]
  - Never   [4]   [ ]

PUB_CLN

☐

	For office use only.
Please put a tick [✓] in ONE box only ...	

21.   Whilst doing your job, have you ever been:
- Insulted verbally   [1]   [ ]
- Assaulted physically   [2]   [ ]
- Both of these   [3]   [ ]
- Neither of these   [4]   [ ]

ABUSED

22.   Are you:
- Female   [1]   [ ]
- Male   [2]   [ ]

SEX

23.   Are you:
- Less than 30   [1]   [ ]
- 30 – 39   [2]   [ ]
- 40 – 49   [3]   [ ]
- 50 or over   [4]   [ ]

AGE

24.   Are you:
- Single   [1]   [ ]
- Married   [2]   [ ]
- Divorced/separated   [3]   [ ]
- Widowed   [4]   [ ]

MAR_STAT

Thank you for your help.

The results will be made available to you as soon as they have been processed.

Leticia Gaeta
Research Officer
Leicester Environment City
Town Hall (3rd floor)
LEICESTER
LE1 6BF

Tel. (0533) 856734

Index